Pottery Book for Beginners

A Potter's Guide to Sculpting 20 Beautiful Handbuilding Ceramic Projects Plus Pottery Tools, Tips and Techniques to Get You Started

By

Garth Mullins

Copyright © 2021 – Garth Mullins

All rights reserved

No part of this publication may be reproduced, distributed, or transmitted in any form or by any means, including photocopying, recording, or other electronic or mechanical methods, without the prior written permission of the publisher, except in the case of brief quotations embodied in reviews and certain other non-commercial uses permitted by copyright law.

Disclaimer

This publication is designed to provide competent and reliable information regarding the subject matter covered. However, the views expressed in this publication are those of the author alone, and should not be taken as expert instruction or professional advice. The reader is responsible for his or her own actions.

The author hereby disclaims any responsibility or liability whatsoever that is incurred from the use or application of the contents of this publication by the purchaser or reader. The purchaser or reader is hereby responsible for his or her own actions.

Table of Contents

Introduction 8

Chapter 1 10

The Basics of Pottery Making 10

    What is Pottery? 10

    History of Pottery 11

    Benefits of Pottery 12

    Application Areas of Pottery 17

    The Business Side of Pottery Making 19

Chapter 2 38

Terms Used in Pottery Making 38

Chapter 3 42

Pottery Making Tips and Tricks 42

Chapter 4 56

Getting Started with Pottery Making 56

    Tools and Materials 56

    Pottery Clay 56

    Kiln 61

    Pottery Wheel 62

    Pottery Modeling Stand 63

    Potter's Needle 64

    Fettling Knives 65

    Chamois 65

    Sponges 66

    Brushes 66

    Aprons and Towels 66

    Potter's Calipers 67

    Slab Roller 67

    Wooden Ribs 68

    Cut-Off Wires 69

    Ribs and Scrapers 69

    Throwing Stick 69

    Loop, Wire, and Ribbon Tools 70

  Setting Up a Pottery Making Studio 70

  Pottery Making Safety Guidelines 76

  Pottery Forming Techniques 83

Chapter 5 86

Pottery Making Process 86

  Clay Preparation 86

  Wedging 87

Forming 87

Drying 87

Leatherhard 88

Greenware 88

Bisque Firing 89

Glazing 90

Glaze Firing 90

Overglaze Firing 91

Chapter 6 92

Pottery and Ceramic Project Ideas 92

Stilted Bucket 92

Clay Bowl 96

Clay Vase 98

Covered Jar Set 101

Nesting Bowl 104

Citrus Juicer 108

Spherical Teapots 111

Three-Piece Vase 116

Textured Platter 121

Pottery Clay Trays 127

Pottery Cylindrical Pot 129

Coil Pot 134

Pottery Starfish 137

Water Font Clay 142

Slab-Built Pottery Mug 144

Basic Slab Pot 149

Ceramic Plant Pot 154

Clay Plate 157

Clay and Rope Pot 159

Clay Spoon 161

Chapter 7 164

Fixing Common Pottery Mistakes 164

Chapter 8 174

Pottery Making Frequently Asked Questions (Q&A) 174

Conclusion 189

Introduction

Pottery making is an old art with the first records of clay designs going back to 4000 B.C. in Egypt and 3000 B.C. in China.

To begin making a piece of pottery, the potter must put together a ceramic/clay body into a specific object (cup, jug). These could be made either by hand or wheel-thrown techniques and subsequently heating at a high temperature in a furnace to eliminate water from the clay. This gives rise to modifications in molded objects, enhancing their strength to last for a long time while shaping them up.

The process of decorating the clay body can start either before or after firing, but the clay does require some preparations to form a piece of work effectively. The clay preparations may involve pressing the clay using bare hands (kneading), the process that ensures that moisture finds its way evenly through the whole slab.

De-airing is the next stage in the preparatory process when using clay. This can be done either manually via wedging or by using a vacuum machine attached to a pugmill; if the de-airing and de-moisturizing of the clay are complete, the clay's shaping in any possible way to form an object. The object formed is made to dry up, and then it is fired.

Whether you are contemplating getting into ceramics or being an enthusiast, knowing everything about creating and forming ceramic objects is important. Assuming you want to enter into ceramics, knowing the techniques you can employ to come up with the best products will offer great assistance to achieve your goal. If you go into the business of collecting ceramics, knowing the difference between mass-produced and handmade can make an incredible difference.

Chapter 1

The Basics of Pottery Making

What is Pottery?

Pottery is the final result of forming vessels and other objects, including clay and ceramic materials, which are usually heated to make them hard and long-lasting.

It is also known that pottery is created out of ceramics and incorporates different kinds of pottery wares like stoneware, porcelain, and earthenware. Ceramic ware is not pottery unless it is heated and that is when the clay will form.

History of Pottery

One school of thought agreed that the first potters came to be in Mesopotamia in the years between 4,000 and 6,000 BC. This was a revolution and not evolution in the way people of old made items out of clay. The revolution did remove the limitations placed on the long process of using bare hands to mold clay by the ancient people but to have the freedom to explore new forms and new designs.

Pottery has had inherent artistic merit, but when the revolution came with the potter's wheel's arrival, the emphases were drastically changed. Pottery was previously known to serve useful purposes; it is now believed to be serving aesthetic ones.

Previously, archaeologists discovered the earliest types of potter were ostensible without decoration and glaze but that wasn't the case everywhere. Around 6,000 BC, it was found out that some places such as China, Europe, and the Middle East had emerged with different design techniques.

Their designs had made a remarkable impression because their paintings did tell past and original findings of Pharaoh's period in office and highly decorated plates and bowls. Ceramists were highly skilled by the work they produced, which also included the ability to produce animal figures. But these innovations were possible because of the discovery of the potter's wheel.

Benefits of Pottery

Undoubtedly speaking, the art of making pots is mostly seen as satisfying, relaxing, and beneficial. The imaginative and creative art of pottery can calm your mind and make you creative.

In this section, we have compiled the health and overall benefits of pottery you stand to gain.

Check out a few benefits of engaging in pottery.

1. **Eases stress**

Pottery art is a platform that increases our creative skills and reduces stress. Because of the high creativity needed in pottery making, our touch sense is very important.

While this is ongoing, we are usually restricted to little or no distractions from the outside world. As a result of this, our stress level is reduced, and we are more than active in the pottery making game.

2. Increases sociability/openness

Making pots is an act that awakens physical and mental activity, and it is also tagged as the right hobby for people who like to increase their energy.

When you engage in group pottery, you can easily make friends with your fellow potters and share ideas that will push your pots and theirs to appear attractive. This friendliness shown by your fellow potters creates a sense of relaxation and socialization that will help you in your journey through life.

3. Enhances focus

Pottery making lets you escape the fears, apprehensions, and problems of life and pushes you to focus on your creativity. While making pots, it is often difficult to get distracted, especially when setting your mind to make beautiful pots. If you can fully focus on making pots only, you are building and improving your focus, which can help you relax and expose you to more things.

4. Creativity

Creativity is known to be the comprehensive leading benefit of pottery. It is evident in virtually every benefit of pottery because it is the bed-rock of making pots. Without creativity, it isn't easy to achieve any tangible thing in life, including pottery making.

Creativity in pottery is a test of your mental and physical attributes, and this art offers you the platform to reveal your abilities. In pottery, one can easily make something and show the world how good they are.

5. Explore and experiment

Thought about exploring and testing out new things? Pottery helps users explore new creative things, allowing them to test and try out new things. This is very important, especially if we seek to improve our creativity level and enhance our pottery skills.

It is perfect for all ages; which means young and older people can engage in the art and explore, test, and build their creativity.

6. Improves body movement

Pottery helps us to improve our exercise level when carrying out the art. For instance, when we move our wrists, arms, and hands while making pots, we exercise.

This little exercise practiced during pottery is of high importance to our body, especially individuals who experience arthritis in the hands. This is because it encourages dexterity and joint movement.

7. Eliminates pain naturally

When we are stressed, we are likely not to be comfortable in our day to day activities. Because pottery is a hobby that increases self-esteem and reduces pain, the pain we experience as a result of stress can be eased away when we engage in making pots.

So, instead of taking pain killers, you can easily participate in pottery and naturally eliminate your inner pain.

8. Enhances quality of life

Expressing yourself can be easily done by engaging in pottery. Pottery is the perfect way to have an inner connection with yourself by increasing your knowledge and better life.

Venturing into new creative arts, learning new skills and wrapping up new creative arts can help you to a long-lasting commitment to educate yourself and keep up with your productive art.

9. Records memories

Archaeological rooms are known for recuperating old artifacts from civilizations long ago. A few of these captured memories or stored artifacts that have been stored some thousands of years ago are believed to be pottery creations. The simple meaning to this benefit of making pottery is that it has the potential to be stored for a very long time.

As you have with other amazing artifacts, pottery is also a magnificent art that is likely not to go out of existence even in thousands of years to come. So, you shouldn't be bothered about losing it whenever you create an amazing or attractive pottery work.

Asides from creating memories in your home, the completed pottery work can be showcased in museums and other art houses. The interesting thing about this benefit is that the next set of generations will also stop by and marvel at your amazing art.

10. Increases positivity level

Pottery allows for enhancements in impulsiveness and flow. It also provides a platform for happiness and helps you identify yourself while also seeking to boost your self-esteem and confidence level.

During the pottery process, your positivity level is always high because there is nothing you can't achieve by creating beautiful and attractive artworks.

Application Areas of Pottery

Pottery is well-designed, of different colors and sizes, and when used for decoration in the home, is quite impressive. Pottery products are used worldwide but might not be in the same and for the same reasons.

But before we dwell on how pottery is made and the stages it goes through in its development to the end product, let us see its usefulness in the home and what use, on average, can people all over the world put it into.

Let us get to see how people use pottery in their homes:

Pottery Bowls

Pottery comes in large and small bowls. Pottery bowls are fantastic for serving food and can be great for day-to-day use and special occasions. However, not all meals can be served with pottery bowls, such as salads, desserts, soups, etc. The choice is now made between big and small bowls and what food is to be served.

Because of the materials used in its production, pottery bowl tends to be more environmentally friendly than other kinds of bowls. It means that harmful chemicals that can come in contact with your food and put your health at risk are likely to be absent. The only underlying problem is likely to be space that ceramic bowls can take up compared with plastic bowls.

It has also been noticed that pottery bowls can make your kitchen more colorful and your kitchen environment better-looking.

Pottery Plates

The beauty of these sets of plates, cups, saucers, mugs, bowls, etc., is that they are a sight to behold when stacked on the kitchen cabinet. The only snag with pottery is that they are breakable, and if handled by a lousy member of the house, breaking of the plates will be more than what will otherwise be.

Vases

Pottery vases can be used to decorate the kitchen apart from other uses they can be put into, and if properly done, can give a magnificent view.

The Business Side of Pottery Making

Pottery is sure to be one of the best hobbies one can engage in and turn into a business. The business side of pottery does not need you to invest a large amount of money or even deep creative skills.

To turn your pottery skills into a business, you need to know about making pots, purchasing the needed equipment, and knowing the nitty-gritty about pottery. Once you can achieve the above requirements, you are only moments away from making pots and selling to the public as a side or full-time business.

Now that you have gotten a very good business idea that can sky-rocket your income in no time, the subsequent step is to proceed to know how you can engage in the business side of pottery making.

Before we get started, it is important to know that starting a pottery business goes beyond just registering the business; you need to know what it entails to succeed and maintain your business success.

Not to worry because we have compiled the right information that will guide you in your journey to make a substantial amount of money every month or annually from pottery:

1. Plan and strategize your business

A detailed and clear strategy is important to succeed as a pottery entrepreneur. Furthermore, the detailed plan and strategy will help you list all your business's needs and requirements, including the less compulsory ones.

Some of the essential questions to ask yourself as you plan and arrange a strategy for your business includes:

- Which market are you targeting?
- What name will be given to your business?
- What amount do I need to start the business and keep it running?
- What price are you willing to charge your potential customers?

Fortunately, we have taken the time to consider the above questions and provide a detailed answer to each of them. Check below for the detailed answers to the above questions:

Which market are you targeting?

Virtually every customer will choose to purchase less costly pottery items widely made available to the public. People who purchase handmade pieces are grateful for the skill and time it took to create a pottery design, and they are most likely to pay additional cash to get a particular pottery piece.

As a matter of fact, these types of people are the ones you should target whenever you are looking for ways to showcase your pottery artifacts. It is important not to target a bad market, or else you risk not selling your pottery works.

What name will be given to your business?

Selecting the right name is very crucial in making pottery sales. Just as important it is, choosing the right name for your pottery business is also very difficult to achieve.

Picking a name for your pottery business is dependent on whether you are operating a one-man business or a partnership business.

On one hand, if you are managing a one-man business, you may want to run your business under a business name instead of your personal name. Look below to see some of the ways to arrive at your business name:

- Social media platforms
- Your state business past record
- Web domain availability
- State and federal trademark record

NOTE - It is necessary and crucial to obtain your domain name before another individual secures it.

What amount do I need to start the business and keep it running?

Before venturing into any business, including the pottery business, the most important thing to consider is the start-up cost. The capital is important in your pottery business because it sets the tone for a small, medium or large business.

A small capital will either mean a small or medium business, while a large amount of capital will mean an intending large business. Some of the questions you need to ask yourself before planning the cost include:

- Electricity – is there a need for an alternative power supply if there is a power failure?
- Studio – Will the studio be built by hand or have a wheel throw?
- Do you want to carry your pots for glazing and firing somewhere else, or will you do so in your home?
- What amount of space do you need for the kiln?

You can start your pottery business in your garage, studio space, or in a shop. Most people prefer to invest or pay for a pottery space away from their homes because it makes them committed to their business. However, not everyone can do so because of the extra cost of getting a space.

Whichever one you may choose to get, the cost still has to be made. After purchasing your space for work, you also have to get some equipment and tools. Some of the equipment and tools include:

- Decorating and carving tools
- Clay
- Work table
- Colorants and glaze

- Wheel (You can purchase wheels from $950 - $1800)
- Business cards
- Kiln (Computerized or manual, and they can be purchased from $2,000 – more than $10,000)
- Display and storage shelves (You also need to get a place to keep damp materials)
- Pug mill (Purchase pug mills from $2,300 - $8,400)

In terms of the above equipment, you cannot do without clay. Also, the kind of equipment and materials you need solely depends on the type of pottery design you want to make.

While starting a pottery business, it is compulsory to get pottery wheels and a kiln. Simply create a list of the complete tools you want and verify the prices from your local art store or online before deciding to purchase them. Do not also forget to have a separate cost for water because you will need lots of it.

When it comes to running a pottery business, the things to consider and keep your mind on is rent, water, electricity, and possibly insurance. Asides from that, you can choose to open a website and get someone to manage it.

What price are you willing to charge your potential customers?

The prices you should charge your potential customers will vary depending on the pottery piece you are selling. Some pottery designs cost way more than others, so you need to consider this when selling to potential customers.

For instance, a pottery design that costs more to create will certainly be highly valued and placed at a high price. The time spent and materials used are crucial in determining the true cost of a pottery design.

While starting, ensure you do not underrate yourself by selling your pottery design less than it should cost. If you do so, you may be giving the impression to your potential customers that your pottery design is not good enough.

How can a pottery business make a profit?

This is pretty much an easy question. Basically, every business makes a profit from the product or value they can offer intending customers.

Pottery businesses simply make a profit from each profit design they sell. Depending on the pottery business owner, you may choose to sell as wholesale or to one-on-one customers.

It does not matter the route you choose to follow; you only have to watch and take the price into serious consideration because it determines if you will sell. If your price is bang on average or it's considered with top-quality designs, you are sure to sell well.

How much money can a pottery business owner gain?

New potter business owners may likely earn below $20,000 in a year. This is necessary because they are just starting out in the business. However, for experienced or skilled potters, they might likely earn an average of $47,500 every year.

Before a novice or new potter can start earning the latter amount, he/she must have been in the pottery business for about 3-5 years.

How can a potter make his business very profitable?

Most master, experienced, or skilled potters have this information at their disposal. Meanwhile, for new potters, they can make their pottery business very profitable by incorporating the following pottery business plan:

- Educating or organizing pottery classes for intending potters like you
- Selling snacks or wine while organizing the pottery classes. In this way, you may likely have your students purchasing the snacks and wine whenever they are on break.
- Building molds. This permits you and your pottery students to create additional pottery designs.
- Calling on other groups to glaze or paint your incomplete work. Once they do so, you can provide them with the chance to go with the completed work, which will serve as a souvenir.
- Making easy a few of your additional detailed pieces and experiment with them to know how they are likely to sell or command the market. Supposing the detailed pieces are found in other pottery stores, you must lessen the number of difficult items and up your game.
- Teaming up with other experienced and well-skilled artists around your environment. Doing so will expose you to learning new things from

skilled and talented artists. It is also a perfect way to market your pottery pieces and get the trust of other great artists.
- Creating pottery designs that attract the general markets. In this step, you need to be as versatile as possible to succeed in your pottery business and any other business you have in mind.
- Asking hotels, bars, real estate agents, galleries, and restaurants to help marketing your pottery designs. This may be a difficult task for many potters because of their nature, but it is a perfect way to market your pottery design and make more money.

2. Create a legal entity

The popular business structure includes the sole proprietorship, corporation, limited liability company (LLC), and partnership.

Building a legal business entity like a corporation or limited liability company protects you and your pottery business from being held responsible if your pottery business gets into legal trouble.

As you have with other business structure kind, starting a limited liability company yourself isn't difficult. You only need to pay the little state limited liability cost or employ a business formation service for a little extra fee.

NOTE – You have to hire a registered agent for your limited liability company if that is what you seek to do. This is because limited liability company's formation packages feature a free year of registered agent services. Through this method, you can choose to stay on your own or employ a registered agent.

For instance, in the USA, the legal process and the filing fees to operate a newly established business are different depending on the state you are in. First of all, a sole proprietorship kind of business means producing and selling your pottery design on your own. In a sole proprietorship business, you don't have anyone under you as you are operating alone.

In view of a limited liability company, it is a legal entity that gets taxed on its own and includes a diverse tax identification number. In the real sense, you won't have a say in selling the pottery design, but the limited liability company will take full responsibility for that.

To find what business structure type is perfect for you, simply contact your tax advisor or CPA.

3. Register to get taxed

You cannot operate a legal business without getting taxed, or else you want to risk having your business being locked up by the state government and paying a huge amount of money to re-open it.

4. Launch a business bank account and possibly a credit card

Every business owner should have a bank account and business credit card. Using your personal bank account and credit card is never advisable when launching a business like pottery.

You need a new bank account and credit card to protect your personal asset. Mixing your personal and your business bank account and credit card is also not advisable because it places your personal assets at risk of your business being legally sued. This is known as piercing your corporate veil in business law.

Also, knowing the process or curating business credit can greatly help you obtain credit cards and additional financing in your business name, high lines of credit, improved interest rates, and others.

Advantages

- It allows for easy tax filing and accounting
- It differentiates your business assets from your personal assets. This is very important to protect your personal asset.

Obtaining a business credit card has the following benefits

- It builds your business credit history. In turn, it is helpful, especially if you want to increase investment and money later.
- It further helps you to differentiate and put apart business and personal expenses.

5. Set up your business accounting

This step is just as important as all other steps. Setting up your business accounting helps you keep track of all expenses and income regarding your pottery business. IIf you can keep track of your annual tax filing, profit, and expenses, you are sure not to run bankrupt.

6. Get the required licenses and permits

Would you want your pottery business to crumble and fall down the drain because of the failure to obtain the required licenses and permits? Certainly, you wouldn't. Why wait for the tax force to visit and lock up your company when you can easily obtain the necessary licenses and permits.

Not obtaining these requirements can force you to pay a huge amount of money as fines to re-open your business once again. Visit your local or state government area to obtain the necessary licenses and permits to run your business without interruption.

Obtain a certificate of occupancy

Usually, a pottery business is run in a studio, especially when tutorial sessions are going on. All businesses working away from a physical location majorly need a certificate of occupancy. This certificate verifies that all zoning laws, government rules, regulations, and building codes have been reached.

Check below if you seek to rent a location:

- In this case, the landlord or owner of the location must get the certificate or occupancy.
- Before hiring a location, ensure that the said landlord has obtained a valid certificate or occupancy linked to your pottery business.
- Once the landlord has completed a deep renovation, a fresh certificate or occupancy will have to be obtained. Also, assuming your pottery business location is renovated before launch, you should add language in your hire agreement, revealing that the hire payments will not begin until your landlord secures a valid certificate of occupancy.
- Asides from hiring a location, if you are building or buying a location space, you will be held responsible for securing a valid certificate of occupancy.

7. Obtain a business insurance

As you have with other top businesses, business insurance is also needed to run your business lawfully and safely. Given any unforeseen and unfortunate incident, business insurance will protect your pottery business and cover any loss that may ensue.

You can find various kinds of insurance policies formed for different kinds of businesses that have different risks. Assuming you are not sure of the risk type that your business is likely to face, simply start with general liability insurance.

Pottery owners can also choose to get workers' compensation insurance because it protects workers whenever a sad situation comes up.

8. Create your brand

You cannot succeed in any business, including the pottery business, without having a brand. Your brand shows how far and how well the public sees your business. If your brand is a strong one and popular, it will lead while other competitors will seek to overpower you.

Marketing and promoting your pottery business

Starting and becoming successful in any business requires you to market and promote the right way. Making sales is one of the biggest challenges every entrepreneur and business owner will face when starting. Still, it can be solved with the right marketing strategy and adequate promoting strategy.

You have tons of options in the traditional marketing way and digital/online marketing and promotion of your pottery business. You can build a list of the major and least markets for selling your pottery designs and create a strategy or plan around it.

We have compiled some promotion and marketing strategies that have helped other high-selling potters out there:

- Pay to get a billboard to show either temporary or permanently at strategic places within your company area. In the billboard, ensure you add your contact details, brand name, motto, and short information to persuade customers to visit your pottery company.
- Endeavor to have a guest book from every event you attend. You can also build a mailing list and deliver mails to people while keeping them reminded of their order or potential orders.

- Another smooth marketing and promoting strategy is to send out pictures of your pottery design on social media sites, including Facebook, Twitter, Instagram, and others. Many talented pottery artists have succeeded in selling their designs online.
- Visit art festivals. Although attending art festivals can be time-consuming and expensive, it is still a very good way of auctioning your pottery design and getting good money out of it. Visiting art festivals will also expose you to meeting more people who will possibly buy your work or refer you to the right people.
- With your mailing list, endeavor to remind customers of the launch or kiln. This means that customers can visit your studio and buy pottery once it comes out of the kiln.

9. Get your business online

The internet is the best place to market your pottery business online. You can pay or design a website yourself where intending customers can read and know certain things about your business and the pottery designs you sell.

Furthermore, you can choose to use social media sites like Twitter, Facebook, or Instagram to draw new customers' attention and keep the existing ones.

Chapter 2

Terms Used in Pottery Making

As a pottery beginner or professional, you need to get acquainted with the necessary terminologies used in pottery making. This will help you easily identify with other potters and know how to better your pottering making business.

Check below for the common terms used in pottery making

1. **Alumina:** This is a key part of the chemical composition of glazes, clay bodies and clays.
2. **Ball clay:** This is another kind of clay taken away from the original rock. It is majorly mixed with other minerals and clays. In ball clays, you can find organic matter. They also dry fast and have a high plastic structure.
3. **Bloating:** This is the everlasting rising of a ceramic while firing is ongoing. It is as a result of the change of gases.

4. **Candling:** This is the reduced temperature part of a few firing cycles. It is majorly used to finish the ware drying.
5. **Carbonizing:** This is the lasting staining of ceramic material by bringing up carbon particles while firing.
6. **Clay:** This is a popular terminology known by most potters. In simple terms, clays are used to make pottery designs.
7. **Clay body:** The clay body is the material that is acted to create the body of a piece of pottery. Consequently, a potter may prefer to purchase a large amount of stoneware body, earthenware body from a ceramic supplier.
8. **Coiling:** This is a hand method of creating pottery designs by simply raising walls using coils of clays that looks like a rope.
9. **Chamotte:** This is a ceramic material created by the high-temperature firing of refractory clay. After firing, it is then blended and crushed to small sizes. Chamotte is used as a non-plastic part of a few clay bodies.

10. **Crocker:** This is another term used to describe a potter.
11. **Delftware:** This is a light pottery body enclosed with a box glaze with overglaze decorations in cobalt on the non-fired glaze.
12. **Earthenware:** This is a pottery design or idea formed by firing the clay with low or reduced temperature.
13. **Fat clay:** A plastic creation of clay. An example includes ball clay.
14. **Dettling:** This excludes a yet to be fired clay body when forming a pottery design. Examples may include edges and seams.
15. **Firing:** This is a term mostly used by all potters. It is the process of heating the soon-to-be pottery design in a kiln to make the clay body mature or come out well.
16. **Fusion:** It is the attaching of glaze and clay surfaces while firing is ongoing in thin joint layers.

17. **Potter's gauge:** This is a tool used to ensure that discarded pots have the same shape and size.
18. **Glaze:** A glaze is a coating that has been heated up to reach the glassy form. It can also mean the mixture or material where the coating is produced or formed.
19. **Glaze firing:** It is a firing spot in a kiln to your desired temperature. During this process, the glaze materials will melt to create a glass type of surface coating.
20. **Kiln:** This is a furnace meant for firing ceramics.
21. **Luting:** A process of attaching two pieces of hard leather clay using a slip.

Chapter 3

Pottery Making Tips and Tricks

Although pottery's craft has several advantages, a few people shun picking this craftsmanship, believing that it's a difficult task. Nonetheless, it would help if you remembered that once you become used to the tips and strategies, it is highly unlikely that it will remain difficult.

Thus, we will give a couple of pottery tricks and tips that can help people who are eager to give their hands a shot at this art.

1. Be comfortable

The first thing you need to deal with when you attend your first pottery lesson is wearing comfortable clothes and feeling comfortable, not the vogue ones, as you will contact clay while creating pots. What's more, if you wear fashionable clothes, they can get dirty, and you might damage them. Thus, consistently ensure you are comfortable with what you wear.

Here are some hints concerning clothes that you can wear during your pottery session:

- Wear clothes that are comfortable, for example, comfortable jeans or pants.
- Ensure pottery clay doesn't ruin your clothes.
- Try not to wear anything excessively loose, particularly in case you're working close to a furnace.
- Ensure your feet are covered and wear fitted shoes and not tight ones.

2. Try not to hope to be perfect at the initial pottery designs

Indeed, making pottery designs is anything but a simple assignment. Pottery is an art that requires standard and consistent difficult work and persistence. You are not going to make astounding designs immediately; it will take a while.

The movements are always difficult to copy with regards to pottery. If you enjoy a pottery class, you will presumably see your teacher create pottery designs like it's so easy.

Nonetheless, it is not so difficult. The real explanation for your tutor's easiness is that they have been doing it for such countless years, and they are accustomed to doing it. In this way, never get disappointed and lose interest; continue creating pottery designs and being patient.

Below are the major issues that you ought to follow if you need to become a pottery professional:

- Do not expect too much, particularly in the first place.
- Have the desire and willingness to learn something new in every pottery class.
- Attempt to keep your dissatisfactions under control

Suppose you expect too much in the beginning, for example. In that case, you believe you will create attractive pottery designs immediately, or you will be the next rated potter, you will end up detesting this lovely craftsmanship.

Instead, you should have the desire to show improvement over the last time, and regardless of whether it's simply figuring out how to move your hands a little bit toward every path in a diverse way, you will improve. Nevertheless, it will take a while, and if you continue trying the difficult work, you will be going to accomplish your pottery objectives.

3. Study clay tossing methods

In case you are truly experiencing difficulty with pottery in the initial stage, you should join a wheel-tossed pottery session. Look for different pottery classes close to you and pick the best one.

While you can tour the web and get familiar with the methods by reading ceramic contents or watching recordings, if you join a class, you will have the option to meet top specialists who can assist you with their experience. Additionally, your tutor will also enlighten you regarding your missteps and help you become a better potter.

You can discover pottery classes at different spots, including:

- Art studios
- Community colleges
- Community center

- Pottery organizations
- Ceramic organizations
- General art locations

Aside from this, you ought to likewise remember your spending plan. A few pottery classes expect you to purchase all that you require for it; however, if you're going to a studio, it might be a less-costly choice because they may have all the materials ahead of time.

Ordinarily, you will most likely need to get together for two or three hours every week with a class that you will need. Ideally, you can locate one that gives you the basic materials you require, and from that point, you will have the option to learn pottery.

4. Clay can be restored

Presently, suppose that you make something excellent and something appears to be wrong somewhere, or possibly, you are evaluating something that you needed to check whether it would work, yet it ends up being a calamity. Now, numerous potters get frightened and begin disliking the pottery activity.

Be that as it may, you ought not to do this since it happens with everybody, even with experts. Besides, pottery sets aside some effort and time to learn. It is not an art you will fully comprehend immediately on your first attempt. Not like the different types of sculping, you can always refurbish clay.

Suppose your clay design is all messed up; there are a ton of things that you can do, including:

- Work the parts that need to be corrected
- Re-structure it
- Make another shape
- Twist it up
- Amend it once more

If you work with a piece of clay on the wheel at the initial period and it turns to be a disaster, is it an opportunity to simply totally surrender this? Not under any condition.

You can wad and revamp the work if you have a feeling that you need to do so. It is the most awesome aspect that any expert potter looks forward to. Regardless of whether you mess it up, you can generally correct it before firing so that if it needs a few kinks to be erased, you definitely can do that.

Other than ruining by framing a bad surface or inaccurate design of your clay piece, another issue that you may confront concerning clay is rock solidifying it. Assuming you are an amateur potter, you may get amazed if you discover your clay has turned stone hard.

Here are a few strategies that can breathe life into your clay once more.

- **Rubbing and moistening**: If your clay is halfway hard, knead it over and over for quite a while, and put it into a fixed impermeable plastic sack by showering some water into it. Sit tight for quite a while, remove it, and knead the clay once more.
- **Drenching into water**: Put the stone-hard clay into a bowl or vessel and add some water to drench it until it becomes useable once more.
- **Adding clay softener:** You can find a few clay softeners in the market that you can use to apply on your clay and knead it until it turns out to be soft.

5. Consider cleanup time

When you work with clay, alongside water, it makes a really bad surface and texture. It is crucial to tidy up your work environment whenever you are finished with your pottery design.

There are a couple of things that you should remember when you're tidying up pottery. See below for some of them:

- Always use a wipe to clean surfaces and trap clay pieces
- Place the too much clay back into the storage space
- Ensure all pottery equipment and tools are cleaned and dried before round up
- Ensure that you clear up the used places before leaving the studio or the pottery class

It's essential to ensure that all these are carried out. You need to ensure that you have everything taken care of because it eases the stress of cleaning it at another time.

The purpose for it is that the clay contains silicate, and when it turns to dust and you inhale, it can cause havoc to your lungs.

6. Practice at home

One thing that you will likewise need to look into when you're making pottery designs is doing so at home. While classes important and advisable, however, in case you're just working with classes, you need to ensure that you're not zeroing in on this as it were.

With regards to rehearsing at home, there are a couple of ways you can carry this out. They include the following:

- Clear a separate room where you will be making pottery, as well as a little kiln. It doesn't need to be large.
- Set up a large area that works for you, perhaps devoting the garage or a large space.

The last option is if you really want to do this at home, and you need the space. Yet, if you have a piece that perhaps you need to work on at home, you can wrap it, take it home, and from that point, you'll have the option to deal with this. It's an excellent method to improve with clay. Generally, take as much time as necessary and figure out how to do this at home and in class.

7. Make the most of your experience

You ought to likewise try to appreciate and enjoy the experience. You should not engage in pottery with the inclination that you need to hit the nail on the head immediately.

That is a typical error many individuals will, in general, make. It's because of how we are trying to ensure we do not make any mistakes for our whole life. Yet, if you have this kind of attitude, you're simply going to upset yourself. Be patient and ensure you do have the right attitude going forward.

Below are several hints to assist you with this.

- Try not to be stressed
- Assuming you commit an error, consider it to be a misstep, and don't stress over it
- Continue to move along, and support the clay motion, however, don't get hung up on errors

- Inhale profoundly every time you are stressed or restless about the experience
- Don't forget why you want to learn pottery

Remembering the entirety of this at whatever point you're working in the studio can greatly improve things and help you become pottery professional. Enter the art with a solid mindset for your very own prosperity and the achievement of you solely dominating the art

8. Purchase your supplies

You ought to consider getting your supplies too. Assuming you purchase your pottery supplies, you can make pottery designs at home

A few pottery classes allow you to bring home the supplies. However, not all places permit that. Besides, whenever you're done, you may need to give it back, yet if you are serious about learning pottery, you should begin to invest the energy forward and begin to get the materials needed.

Meanwhile, you need to ensure that you are purchasing what you need for the pottery activity. Purchase the things that you feel the best fit for you and your expertise level.

Insignificantly, here are the most important things to get:

- Pottery area
- Kiln
- Wheel
- Clay

Asides from the above-listed tools and needs, other requirements are not compulsory for beginners, but they offer a great deal of help if you seek to raise your expert level.

Start with the listed ones, and you will be surprised to see the level you have reached under a short period with consistent practice both at home and at the pottery class.

9. Get appropriate information on your equipment or tools

Pottery activity is all about adhering to the right tips and tricks. While using the available supplies, you should turn out to be quite acquainted with the tools. Without knowing the idea of the tool with which you will work, you won't ever have the option to oversee them appropriately. Along these lines, it's vital to be acquainted with the characteristics of the tools or equipment that you will use. For example,

- Clay: The major and significant material for creating any pottery design is clay. Thus, you should be aware of the clay idea first. There are various kinds of clays accessible in the craft store.

A Short message from the Author:

Hey, I hope you are enjoying the book? I would love to hear your thoughts!

Many readers do not know how hard reviews are to come by and how much they help an author.

I would be incredibly grateful if you could take just 60 seconds to write a short review on Amazon, even if it is a few sentences.

\>> Click here to leave a quick review

Thanks for the time taken to share your thoughts!

Chapter 4

Getting Started with Pottery Making

Tools and Materials

Potter's newbie should be aware of the different tools and equipment required to make pottery, together with the different techniques and materials. Meanwhile, we will concentrate on the equipment necessary to make pottery.

Pottery Clay

This is a delicate earth when it is wet and rigid when it is dry. It is usually formed and heated to make things, for example, pots and blocks.

Types of clay used in pottery making:

1. Stoneware
2. Ball Clay
3. Porcelain
4. Fire Clay
5. Earthenware

There are numerous kinds of pottery clay that can be utilized for making clay designs.

It is important to equip yourself with some answers to the essential questions to know your pottery designs' best clay body.

How to choose the right pottery clay

Answer the following questions when you are seeking to choose the right pottery clay for your pottery craft:

1. **What kind of pottery are you most comfortable with?**

The kind of pottery clay you need to make immensely affects the type of clay you pick. For instance, a few mud bodies are extraordinary as tossing clays. However, it would be a calamity as a hand building mud for an outside design. You might also discover that you need to utilize additional clay bodies, and it is always seen as the best plan.

2. **What tool is accessible to you?**

While it's feasible to create completed ceramics totally by use of the hand, this requires a lot of measure of exertion and time. Utilizing equipment assists in talking less of your strength energy for what you need to do most.

The three major potters tools are the ones meant for handling, firing, and shaping. Regardless of whether you have these tools, it will affect the clay you will utilize.

Types of clay processors:

- Equipment for wedging and for hand mix
- Clay blenders
- Pugger-mixers
- Pugmills

Types of shaping equipment:

- Extruders
- Slab rollers
- Potter's wheels

You can fire in a kiln through the following ways:

- Are you in possession of a kiln?
- Can you gain entry to kilns by entering classes?
- Is it possible to hire a kiln?

How to find pottery clay

1. From road cuts
2. From construction sites
3. From river banks
4. From stream beds

3. What temperature can I fire to?

The duo of glazes and pottery clay should develop at a similar temperature to forestall problems in the completed piece. There are three essential temperature ranges (with little variation among singular potters). The development temperature identifies with the cone rating of a given mud body or coating:

- Low-Fire: Cone 06 to Cone 3 (1,850–2,135 degrees F)
- Mid-Reach: Cone 4 to Cone 7 (2,160–2,290 degrees F)
- High-Fire: Cone 8 to Cone 10 (2,315–2,380 degrees F)

4. Purchase soaked pottery clay

Commercially accessible soaked pottery clay presents a helpful method to purchase mud on the off chance that you are without the machines to blend it yourself. This is particularly valid for the muds that are handled utilizing a de-broadcasting pug plant, which takes out a ton of crafted by wedging the clay.

Blending clay by yourself has some benefits. The initial point is based on financial: soaked clay offers significantly more than dry mud, and it is seen in delivery costs. Another benefit of blending your own is that you can utilize custom pottery clay plans and alter them as you want.

5. Test with pottery clays

Perhaps the ideal method to discover clays that are ideal for your necessities is to try different things with different pottery clays. Attempt purchasing different types of a few clay types that appear to be the thing you are searching for.

Endeavor to go with every clay, going towards the boundary, and create notes of what you are thinking and what you notice on paper.

Likewise, you can make experiment pieces, for example, tiles, chimes, or bowls, and heat them as per a standard heating plan.

Kiln

The basic and main piece of equipment you need to get the pottery craft off to a good start is a kiln. The kiln is like an oven where pottery is made solid. Accumulated clay has to be loaded on a kiln under a high temperature of up to 1800 degrees F.

If the temperature is lower, the wares may not be as solid as they should be and should not last for too long before eroded. So this single device is important for firing and baking glazes onto the pottery. Without this piece of equipment, you can't create things such as pots or vases.

Those potters that are well established use different firing equipment that may include commercial-grade wood, gas kilns and electricity. However, as a newbie, it is necessary to begin using a kiln that is easy to manage, like an electric-powered "hobby" kiln that can hit a maximum temperature of 2340 F

The kiln can range from a simple piece of equipment that can easily be plugged into a wall outlet, while larger kilns may need to be installed by an electrician and possibly need a regular service. As far as procurement cost is concerned, the small, simple operated kiln can cost a few hundred dollars while a more sophisticated kiln can be obtained up to a few thousand dollars.

Pottery Wheel

A pottery wheel is a piece of equipment that gives shape to the clay while spinning. It all depends on the

level you want to operate; if you are into highly developed ceramic pieces, you will surely need a more sophisticated potter's wheel. The wheels have two types – electric operated and manually operated. Your pottery wheel choice should now depend on what you consider the advantages and disadvantages of your scale of operation.

A newbie rolling out pottery on a small electric wheel makes business sense since it doesn't need the sophisticated coordination necessary to kick the wheel while a shape is being formed. In addition, the electric wheel provides more torque and speed control to help manage the clay. Besides, it is rugged and has high capacity; it has been estimated that one wheel can create more than 500,000 mugs before going for repairs.

On the other hand, the manually operated wheels can be flexible as it allows the user more control than its electrical counterpart. The wheels' full control is made possible because the speed of the wheel totally depends on how much they kick the wheel with their foot.

Pottery Modeling Stand

If you decide to toe the part of the manual method of producing pottery, you can also consider bringing in a pottery molding stand since it eases the creation process. It simply requires the potter to place their slab of clay on the rotational surface area, with the attendant simplicity to form.

Main Tools for pottery production

You will need a certain number of tools, but they are not as crucial as the equipment mentioned above; nevertheless, they are important if you want to produce the kind of pottery you desire. In fact, if you decide to do away with special tools, your bare hands can execute the job. But several tools can give your pottery production a lease of life, cushion the process, deliver a better product, and help you in the expansion drive.

Potter's Needle

These are tools that look like long needles and are specially designed for trimming edges on a wheel or scoring slabs of clay for hand throwing applications.

Fettling Knives

These knives are used to trim the wire to the desired angle and curve cuts. There are two types of fettling knives –soft and hard knives. Soft fettling knives are flexible and can be bent into different shapes, while hard fettling knives are inflexible but useful for making clean, straight cuts.

Chamois

Chamois is used to smooth the rim of pots or compress edges of thrown ware; these tools are of great importance.

Sponges

These are important tools, particularly when you are working at the potter's wheel. Sponges are very useful in absorbing and distributing water during throwing, with the result that the molding and shaping of the clay are facilitated. Sponges make it easier for water to reach the hard to reach areas of the clay.

Brushes

In the production process, especially when molding clay, brushes are very useful when carrying water and slipping to specific areas. Brushes also are useful when applying paint, whether underglaze or overglaze.

Aprons and Towels

This is really a messy craft, and without the appropriate apron and towels, your clothes will be constantly messy, with the result that it may begin to affect you psychologically. Aprons and towels are important for preventing stains and dirt.

Potter's Calipers

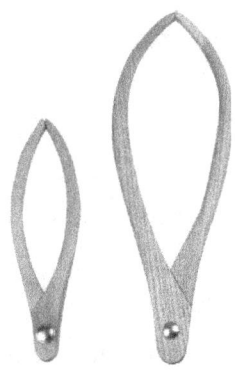

This is a useful tool in measuring the inner and outer dimensions of pots at the point of meeting other parts of a working set.

Slab Roller

Slab Rollers consider brisk and effective creation of clay sections utilized in hand building and chiseling. It also adds to wheel-tossed structures. Mud slab rollers are basically modern measured moving pins -

notwithstanding, the advantages of utilizing a slab roller over are a moving pin are excessive.

One of the major reasons that craftsmen use mud slab rollers is for the even, reliable slabs they can make rapidly. These slabs are perfect for creating tiles, utilizing hump and slump molds, and making other hand-built ceramic products.

Slab rollers can likewise turn out a lot of clay, which would somehow be tough or hard with a handheld moving pin. Furthermore, mud slab rollers are made with the end goal that back agony or strain, which regularly joins moving pieces by hand, can be prevented.

Wooden Ribs

These are materials used to smoothen, press, and straighten clay on the wheel.

Cut-Off Wires

A thin piece of wire is needed to evacuate the piece of pottery from the wheel at completion. The wire can be nylon or metal-based but has wooden notches at both ends for the potter to hold.

Ribs and Scrapers

These pieces of tools do the work of shaping and smoothing the pottery at the formative stage. In coiled pottery, they can also be of help during the rib-and hand technique.

Throwing Stick

This tool facilitates the cleaning process of the outside of pottery pieces. Also, it helps in making an undercut bevel at the base. A bevel helps in cutting the pot from the wheel.

Loop, Wire, and Ribbon Tools

In hand molding pottery, this tool offers flexibility when trimming clay slabs, particularly adopting hand molding in the production process.

Setting Up a Pottery Making Studio

Organizing and arranging your pottery studio will need you to make some spending. However, when you get the required tools, it will keep going for a long time. For the specialist, organizing a workspace be pretty much as straightforward as procuring a wheel, a work table and a little rack unit to store your work. But, for the genuine potter, getting a pottery studio needs a considerable amount of tools.

Before purchasing the required tools, you should figure out where you will actually want your new shop to be located. A few inquiries to consider would be:

- Would I like to make wheel tossed pots or simply hand building?
- Is it compulsory to spot a furnace, and provided that is done, is there a sufficient power supply to the area?

- Do I need to coat my pots in my studio, or is it mandatory to take them elsewhere to coat and fire?

Assuming hand building is the solitary thing you need to do, an additional room in your home would be an ideal spot to set up a little studio. Everything necessary would be sufficient space for a work table (a 4' x 8' table is perfect), a little electric furnace and a rack to store your finished piece and a few tools.

Meanwhile, in terms of a wheel tossing studio, you will require a space adequately enormous to have a wheel, a work table, a clay stockpiling territory, racks to store your work, a sink including sufficient water, a device stockpiling zone, a different space for coating and furnace firing.

Equipment

This section will zero in primarily on setting up a wheel tossing studio that will consider just a little space. The primary piece of equipment we will examine is a potter's wheel.

Wheel

There are numerous wheels available, and they range in cost and quality from modest and feeble to costly and rock-solid expert quality. These wheels cost about $950 and may likely rise to about $1700.

However, they are the acceptable universally handy wheel, appropriate for some extraordinary expertise levels. Assuming you think ceramics is something you won't ever full-time yet will simply do as a pastime, the Brent IE is an ideal wheel.

Work Table

Assuming you have sufficient space, a 4' x 8' sheet of mid-range grade compressed wood covered with substantial material is ideal for a work table. Also, if you are without enough space, cut the sheet of compressed wood down to the size you want and close it with substantial material.

It is vital to extend the material tight and staple it planted on the compressed wood's bottom. At some point, the material may loosen up and should be re-extended over the table. This is a viable work table and makes an incredible surface for getting ready mud or some other work you may have to do, aside from coating.

For coating, you should close your table with plastic. You don't need a coating to get blended in with your clay or stain the tabletop. Preferably, you ought to have a different table for glazing.

Shelf

When your pottery pieces are made, you should have a storage space or shelf to keep them on until you are prepared to fire them. A straightforward wooden shelf functions well.

Damp room

It is extremely useful to have a spot to store moist pieces that actually should be done. An old fridge with racks still in it functions extremely well. Another choice would be a metal or wooden rack with a sheet of plastic cuddle folded over it, so it is completely encased.

Furnaces/Kilns

There are numerous electric furnaces or kilns accessible, yet not all ovens are made the same way. Throughout the most recent years, there has been a developing interest in pottery, and numerous individuals have set up specialist studios at home. Large numbers of them bought the least expensive potential kilns, utilized them for a couple of years and put them away until they chose to sell their tools.

Glaze section

Whether you make your glazes or purchase pre-made powders and blend them yourself, you will require a predetermined area in your studio to keep your glazes and coat your pots. Five-gallon basins with covers function extremely well for holding blended coatings.

You will need to set the cans on a table so they are at an agreeable level for you to work with. Placing them on the ground will be extremely difficult on your back, and having to excessively high of a table will make it hard for you to coat your pots.

Bat Storage

A focal area to keep your bats and equipment is significant. A versatile truck with a rack on top is the best choice, yet any kind of rack with level bars to hold the bats and a rack on top to hold compartments with devices will work.

Clay storage

A decent spot to store a large amount of clay should be under your work table. Furthermore, a straightforward rack raised a couple of creeps off the floor is critical to go below the clay, as any general or cleaning will permit residue or water to gather under your cases or sacks.

Tidiness is significant in your studio. The dirt made from dry clay includes silica and ought not to be breathed in. Perhaps the ideal approach to keep away from extreme dust is not to leave clay leftovers lounging around to evaporate and clean later. Water left on the floor around dirt will make the shape a slipping risk.

Rundown of required tools

Below is the rundown of the essential tools you should begin with:

- Needle tool
- Wire tool: They are useful in scrapping out clay
- Sherrill Mud Tools elastic ribs
- Sponge: They are useful in adding and removing water while working with the clay.
- Wooden blade
- Wooden bowl rib
- Clean up tool
- Trimming tool

- Ruler: This is useful for making your work more precise
- Glazing tongs
- Turntable
- Paintbrushes

Extra Tools

There are a couple of extra tools that are a great idea to have, however not fundamental to begin with.

- Huge bowl rib
- Straightforward cutting tools
- Calipers
- Throwing stick

Pottery Making Safety Guidelines

Ensuring safety in your pottery studio is vital to continuing your life as a potter. In the pottery profession, several likely dangers can cause us pain. Being mindful and taking deterrent measures is the ideal approach to remain protected in the studio as long as possible.

The most effective method to ensure safety in your pottery studio:

1. Try not to allow the clay to sit out

When you allow the clay to sit out to dry and afterward it is brushed, silicate dust can resurface. This issue usually occurs at pottery wheels, where the decorations may be forgotten about and can get very dry over the long run.

It is essential to avoid potential risk and wet the dry mud to catch the silicate dust before it turns airborne and afterward tidies the space.

2. Clean surfaces

Cleaning surfaces will trap dirt before they turn airborne. This is significant for clay particles that happen from cutting down and glaze blending. When there is a lot of dirt, cleaning it with a wet material can trap the dirt and keep you protected from breathing in dirt into your lungs.

3. Carefully store powders

Storing powders in impermeable containers is best for your wellbeing and the life span of the powders. When powders are stored, it keeps you from breathing in the dirt that may have piled up. Another advantage of storing your powders is that it keeps dampness or different toxins from getting blended into the powder and demolishing its uprightness.

4. Have your furnace in a protected area

Having a protected oven area can greatly help extend your kiln and keep it from likely flames. Ensure every flammable material and fluids are taken away from the kiln area to keep flames and blasts from happening. Make sure to utilize metal shelves rather than wooden ones if they are near your oven.

5. Emergency shut off

Having a crisis shut off for furnaces and other controlled tools is significant when things go wrong. A breaker for the furnace can terminate the electric kiln's power when there is a major problem.

6. Clean pottery equipment

Clean pottery equipment is significant for the life span of your equipment and your safety. If you possess a rusted tool and you cut yourself by mistake, you have to be perturbed about having tetanus. This is why you must clean your pottery tools after using any of them.

7. Keep harmful fluids contained

Harmful fluids should be contained in a section when not used to forestall spills and unexpected openness to the fluids.

8. Poisonous vapor get vented

Venting poisonous vapor is vital to remaining in good health in the studio. It tends to be extremely perilous to your well-being to inhale chemicals that can make you ill. Make sure to be protected and utilize a vent and respirator or work outside.

9. Clean always in and out of the studio

Cleaning the studio regularly can assist you with arranging your tools and cleaning clay dust. Long haul openness to silicate dust can make genuine harm your lungs, so tidying up the floors, tables close to the wheels can go far to making you healthy.

10. Venting the studio

Venting the studio can be significant when there is a pile-up from not cleaning the studio. Opening windows and entryways can help eliminate dirt and particles noticeable all around that may harm your health throughout an extended period.

Instructions to keep yourself protected in the pottery studio

1. **Wear a respirator**

Putting on a respirator is vital while carrying out pottery projects in the studio. A respirator can further help you avoid dirt that turns airborne during any of the projects from arriving into your lungs and causing severe harm.

2. **Wear appropriate footwear**

Assuming you don't wear the right footwear, a couple of shut toe shoes, you may get yourself injured in the feet. Dropping tools or furnace furniture can slice your feet up or even break a few bones. Wearing the correct footwear in the pottery studio can go a long way in preventing foot injury.

3. **Deal with wounds**

Dealing with wounds is significant whenever they occur. This may include cuts, wounds, or burns. It is ideal to have an emergency treatment unit in your studio.

Make certain to wear gloves if you have an injury on your hand and take care of clay. When it comes to serious and severe injuries, it is ideal to avoid the studio until you are completely recuperated to guarantee that you don't harm yourself further.

4. Wash your hands consistently

Washing your hands once done with wheel tossing can be exceptionally useful to keep your hands and body free from sickness or bacteria.

Leaving clay on your hands can make your hands dry out and, in the long run, break and cause damage if you don't rub cream.

5. Utilize the right venting

Appropriate venting in the studio can offer great assistance in reducing piled up dust in your studio. Bad substances, for example, gold gloss, should be allowed to open outdoors since they are powerful and can cause cerebral pains.

6. Use appropriate eyewear

Using appropriate eyewear is significant when crushing down a large glaze. Glaze remains can take off from the crushing wheel and enter your eyes if you do not use protective eyewear. Additionally, face shields are a decent choice or alternative option to guard your whole face while granulating down your project's lower part.

7. Monitor your tools

Monitoring your tools is imperative to staying away from likely hand wounds. Make sure to view and verify your basin in the wake of tossing to guarantee that th3 5oolw and wipes don't end up in a pugmill.

8. Drink enough water to remain hydrated

Remaining hydrated in the pottery studio is vital to feeling stimulated and wakeful while designing a pottery project. Assuming you end up tired, you should endeavor to have a go at your water bottle. Being dehydrated can lead to sensations of sickness, faintness, exhaustion, tipsiness, etc. Whether you don't feel like drinking water, it is still important to drink water to guarantee good health.

9. Try not to consume food in the pottery studio

Consuming food in the pottery studio can be unhygienic. You could consume mud or dust by mistake if you are not careful. Moving away from your studio can be a decent break and the best method to keep anything in your studio from entering your food.

10. **Perform exercises**

Performing exercises are essential to ensuring good health as potters. Often, potters twist around a ton from wheel tossing, wedging, working extended periods on projects, etc. Taking a break at regular intervals to get up, stretch, and stroll around can keep you from creating back issues and other spinal issues.

Taking everything into account, the pottery studio is a pleasant spot to be, the place where you can make lovely and stand-out pottery pieces. Nonetheless, it is vital to be protected while in the studio to keep yourself healthy and avoid any health issues.

Pottery Forming Techniques

Regardless of if you are contemplating venturing into pottery or being an enthusiast, being equipped with the methods of creating and forming ceramic objects is important. Assuming you want to venture into pottery, knowing the techniques you can employ to come up with the best products will help you achieve your goal.

If you go into the business of collecting ceramics, being aware of the distinguishing factors between mass-produced and handmade can make an incredible difference. Since you cannot differentiate, it makes sense that before you dabble into the business, you should consult with experienced ceramicists about which methods will be most suitable for you.

Hand-built

These are produced by using hand and tools. They are also made through coil, slab, or pinching.

Pinching

They are regarded as the easiest type of hand-built technique. Pinching is produced by rolling, squeezing your finger until you are satisfied with the design.

Coil

The coil is the basic part of the hand-built technique. Rolling clay and forming coil can produce big pots. Tools are then used to make the pottery design smooth.

Slab

The slab technique describes rolling the clay and making sheets with molds. It is also a very common technique in pottery.

Wheel Thrown

The first potter's wheels were discovered around 3100 BC in Iraq. Potter's wheels make use of force to quickly produce pottery vessels.

Slip-cast

Slip-cast is identified as a large technique of creating pottery. This technique is not included in the handmade one. Also, this method requires you to make a pottery design from liquid clay which is then put into the mold to create a pottery design.

Chapter 5

Pottery Making Process

Clay Preparation

Clay preparation is the first stage in pottery production, and it involves the sourcing of the plastic clay body. A long time ago, the only option opened to potters was to dig for the clay they use from locally available sources. The digging process has not gone away as some potters, including the Native American potters, still do. Through the sourcing of the plastic clay from the mother earth, they feel connected to the earth. Even the Native American potters of the Southwest offer sacrifices for the clay they remove from the earth they use to produce their pots.

Digging the soil in search of the plastic clay makes sourcing the clay very difficult for the urban potters because it demands many physical efforts. As a result, many resorts to buying commercially available clay bodies from suppliers in their area of abode. But they have to pay high prices because the costs associated with shipping are high.

Wedging

When the plastic clay has been procured, the next stage is to begin mixing the clay by hand (wedging) on a table, which includes pressing and rotating the clay ball. The objective is to make sure the clay is thoroughly blended as well as removing all air bubbles. This part of this process is taken seriously since an explosion would occur in the kiln if there are traces of air bubbles in the clay.

When fired in the kiln, the air pockets expand because if there is the presence of air bubbles in the clay, it will burst. If you are careful, you will see the red light in the form of holes in the clay and quickly do something about it before it hits the kiln.

Forming

Once the clay has been mixed very well, different methods may be formed: slab, wheel, coil, pinch, and mold. It is possible to combine these methods, or one of them can be used.

Drying

The drying process begins when the clay bag is opened. The process makes it lose water and get stiffer, and it goes further to shrink. When the pieces you create have formed, they should be wrapped in soft sheets of plastic and be placed on a shelf in a damp room. Placing these pieces in the damp room will slow down the drying process due to the plastic. You must make sure that the pieces you create will have no holes, as the holes will likely cause an explosion when fired.

Leatherhard

Leatherhard is the state of partial dryness, and it is achieved when the pieces wrapped in plastic are kept in a damp room for a few days. At this stage, the pieces stiffen and are no longer flexible. The pieces are now refined by adding handles or other decorative elements, carving out excess clay, trimming the footing of a bowl, etc. It is time to do all the modification and refining of the piece since, after this stage, no further change of the piece can take place.

Greenware

The piece will eventually dry up completely. When it happens, it is referred to as greenware, meaning that all water has been lost via evaporation and it is no longer flexible. An attempt to bend it will cause it to break, and you neither add nor subtract from it. It is ready for the stage of firing.

The dried pieces can now be moved with care out of the damp room to the greenware racks. This piece of work will accumulate to the number required to fill a kiln. Only pieces of work on the greenware carts are eligible to be fired. Others in the damp room will remain until they are moved to the greenware.

Bisque Firing

The next stage in the journey to produce pottery is to take the accumulated dry clay from the greenware and load it onto the kiln to begin the first of two firings. The firing is about 1,800 degrees F. With firing at this degree, it makes the ware hardened and easy to handle without the fear of breaking when it goes through glazing. Firing the clay at this temperature doesn't make it less absorbent, but it retains its porosity.

What goes on in this process is that when the clay is fired, the water in the clay is absorbed by the porous bisque ware, but the glassy materials in the glaze are placed on the surface of the bisque ware. This means that the bisque process is carried out to make glazing stress-free.

The firing of the bisque is done within the space of three days. On the first day, the kiln is laden with dry greenware, after which the kiln is ignited but set at a low level and left overnight to dry the ware and get warm.

However, on the second day, the kiln temperature is gradually increased, and it will keep on rising until it reaches the target of 1,800 degrees F. At this level, the kiln is switched off and allowed to cool slowly. The third day marks the kiln's opening to remove the bisque, which is then returned to the lab as pottery. In the lab, it is placed on the shelf with the inscription "BISQUE WARE."

Glazing

The glazing process begins with a mixture of ground glass, coloring materials, clays and water. The glaze is added to the bisque by dipping, pouring, drenching, coating, scrounging, or combining these techniques. The pots are to be placed on the glaze racks but have to wait until there enough to fill a kiln. It should be remembered that the footing of each piece must be unrestricted of the glaze while the pot is glued to a bisque fired **"cookie."**

Glaze Firing

The firing process takes place within three days. Once the glaze firing temperature of 2350 has reached, the pots are allowed to cool, the day three will see the pots unloaded and stored in the storage room where the rest of the work that has been produced is kept. This is indeed the final step in the series of steps required to make pottery. But there could still be another optional step.

Overglaze Firing

Some potters sometimes prefer to do additional firings to achieve color and surface effects considered impossible in the glaze firing. The additional glaze is fired at an extremely low temperature of 1,300 degrees F. The effects aimed to achieve include lusters, china paints and decals. As a result of the additional glaze, clearer colors and luster can occur than would be possible under the condition of 2,350 degrees F. With the low temperature of 1300 F, it does not melt the main glaze, but the luster, china paint, or decal melt on the glaze and fuse.

The fuse is partly permanent, which the major drawback of this technique. Since the technique is not as permanent as the high-temperature glazes, abrasion will corrode this coating and eventually, the overglaze will disappear with time.

Chapter 6

Pottery and Ceramic Project Ideas

Stilted Bucket

The stilted bucket design is a pottery project idea that allows you to present or offer fruits and other beautiful and attractive things. You wouldn't like to present a gift without presenting it attractively.

Materials

- Clay

Instructions

1. First of all, toss a cylinder without the underside.

2. Spot an equal space grid around the outer part before pressing it using your hands.

3. Use your finger to press out the form.

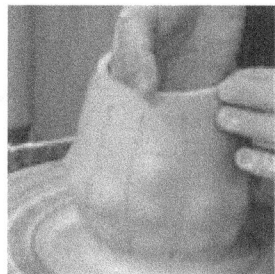

4. Furthermore, also press the clay balls at the meeting of the grid.

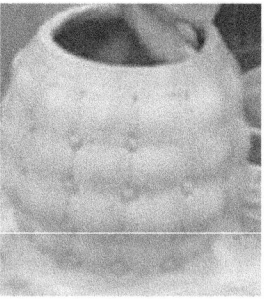

5. Toss a disk and compress it, then form an oval shape with the disk.

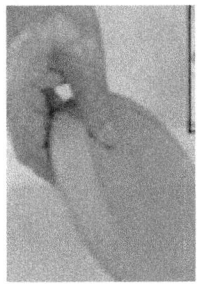

6. Rollover the edges while curving the ends.

7. Toss a wide cylinder with no bottom

8. Cut off excess clay from beneath the clay in step 4.
9. Cut into half and

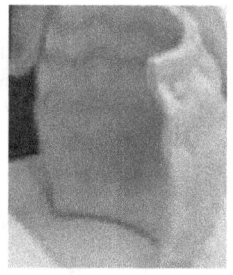

10. Place on a foam and attach its underbelly to the stilts (from step 6)

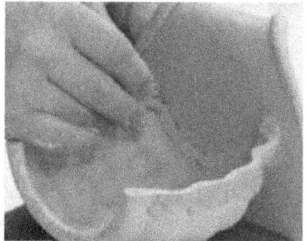

11. Cut out some part of the wide cylinder, and join to it.

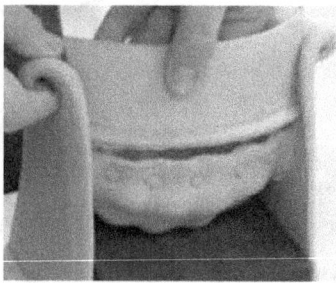

12. Go on to mix the little coils to support the entire attachment, then trim a curve in each

stilt's bottom part and attach handles to the top of the stilts to form your stilted bucket

 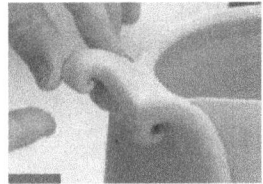

13. Lastly, ensure the final design from step 12 is dried for several days before bisque firing

Clay Bowl

The clay bowl project is an easy clay design idea to create. They are useful for our everyday lives, and they can serve a lot of functions. For example, a clay bowl can be used to keep fruits or any other thing.

Materials

- Paint
- Air-dry clay
- Paintbrush
- Water
- Clay rib

Instructions

1. With your two hands, roll the clay to form an orange-shaped ball.
2. Use your thumb and press the middle of the ball and pinch the clay while turning it with your second hand. Begin close to the underside of the clay and move upwards while still rotating.

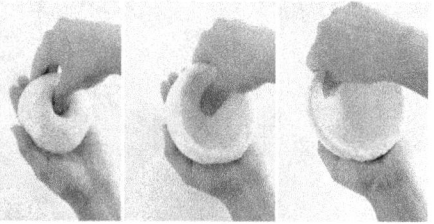

3. The clay rib should be used to make straight the inner and bowl rim. You may also need to use the clay rib to take too much clay on a few sides that appear to have much clay.

4. Position the bowl on flat ground to make straight the lower part.
5. When you have gotten your perfect shape, allow the blow dry for a minimum of one day.

Clay Vase

Clay vases are used to hold or store flowers. Additionally, they are also used to beautify the home, offices and outdoor spaces.

It is an easy craft that does not require too much time to complete, and it is perfect for beginners.

Materials

- Rolling pin
- Sponge
- Craft knife
- Clay
- Wax paper
- Clay carving tools
- Glass bottle

Instructions

1. Roll a large amount of clay into a little ball shape. On the top of your wax paper, simply knead clay into a disc around ¼ inch. Ensure it is rolled into more than one direction.

2. With a craft knife, make sure you carve or cut the clay into a rectangle-shaped glass bottle size and curve it on the sides of the bottle. **NOTE** – The clay will glue to the glass if you use force in this process, so you need to take it gradually.

3. Include clay strips to create the lower part of the vase. Your fingers are perfect for making the joints smooth.

4. Include more clay strips to form a top lip. Also, your fingers will smoothen the surface and attach the creases with a little amount of water. A soaked sponge can level the rough surfaces.

5. From the lower part, slowly move the glass bottle away from the clay vase and arrange any rough part of the clay. Form the underside of the vase by placing it over the clay slab.

6. Furthermore, trim or carve the clay base with a craft knife.
7. Leave the clay vase to dry. This should take about three days, then bisque fire the vase.

Covered Jar Set

The covered jar set design is made up of two jars that are attached using clay. They are used to carry or transport more items from one place to another.

Materials

- Clay

Instructions

1. Toss two similar jars. It is better to use the same jars because it makes the whole process easy.

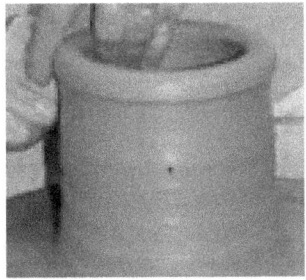

2. Form a gallery for the lid to sit in and create lids using a small inner bevel on the edge.

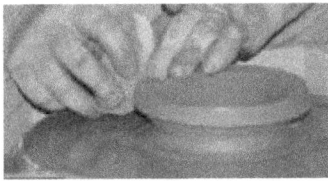

3. Once done with carving, join the created ones by putting a coil in the middle. Then push the two created ones and make the seam smooth.

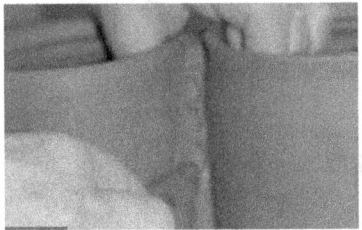

4. Change the position of the attached forms on the top and complete working on the seams.
5. Proceed to roll out a handle and place it across the lids to join with slip. After that, attach the handle until you get your perfect shape.

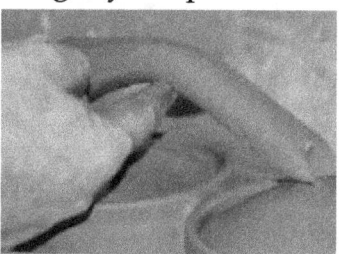

6. Include little coils to finish the attachment between the handle and lid before adding lugs and closing it a bit to ensure the moisture can come out.

7. Extend the handle and leave it for some days to prevent cracking, then fire in a kiln. You can design the jar set however you choose to.

Nesting Bowl

This is another special type of clay bowl used for the storage of food or fruits. They are also simple to create; beginners and professionals can choose to make a nesting bowl anytime they want.

Materials

- Pencil
- Clay
- Tart tin

- Knife
- Texture tool
- Foam
- Wet sponge

Instructions

1. Get sharp tart tins with removable lower parts and form a dart template by sketching around the rim.

2. Ensure your bowls nest by using similar dart proportions on every template.

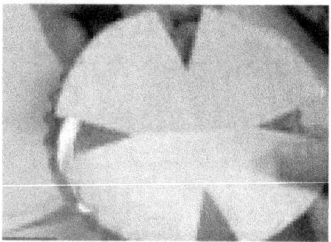

3. Smooth the slab using a soft rib. Ensure at least one inch is left so that you can change anything if there is an issue.

4. Press the clay inside the texture but not too much. Then position a well-arranged texture tool on the slab and turn it with little force.

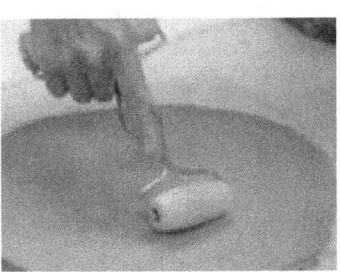 

5. Using your inner bowl face, use the sharp tart tin to carve the slab and cut the darts using the top of the knife on the middle and two sides.

6. Slip the trimmed dart rim and carry the slab to attach the two sides, then clean the rough part with a wet sponge.

7. Position a piece of foam on the bowl edge and flip it to the other side. Work on the lower seams

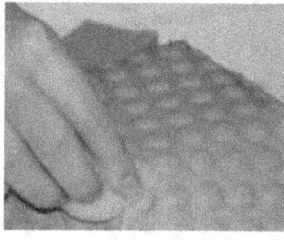

8. Adjust the shape, leaving it to dry.

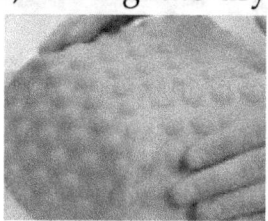

Citrus Juicer

This pottery project idea is simple and quick to create. The finished project is meant for juicing citrus. It can stay for a long period if maintained well.

Materials

- Clay
- Metal tool
- Needle tool
- Loop tool

Instructions

1. Toss about 7-inch clay and open the clay's center.
2. Cut the inner part using a needle tool and pull up the wall of the middle opening.

 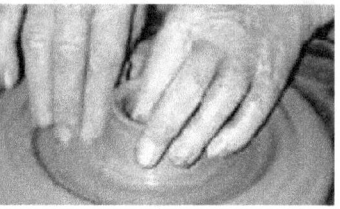

3. Cover the opening and allow for a little blunt tip.

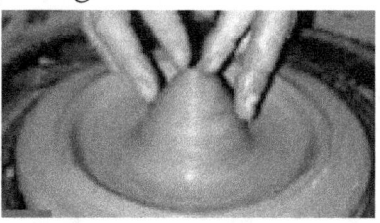

4. Toss the exterior wall and allow for a flat inner lower part.

5. Cut the exterior lower part using a metal tool and round up the edge with a curve before creating any spout type.
6. Flute the middle using a little loop tool.

7. Join your handle.

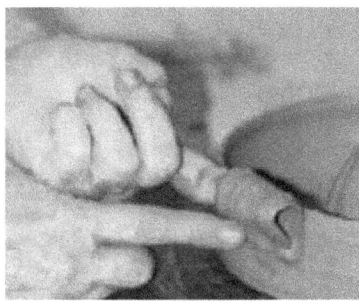

8. Finally, allow it to dry for several hours and sand lightly. Then use a damp sponge to smoothen it.
9. Avoid using thick glazes that could dull the edges of the fluting and the tip.

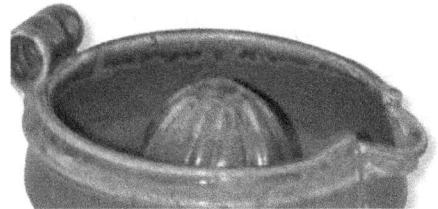

Spherical Teapots

Spherical clay teapots are formed on the pottery wheel, and beginners can explore this opportunity to create one. They serve multiple purposes, including storing water and so much more.

Materials

- Clay
- Toilet paper
- Surform tool
- Styrofoam ball
- Glue
- Metal rib

Instructions

1. Each teapot starts with draping a slab of clay over a plaster hump mold by using a Styrofoam ball and cutting it in half. Styrofoam balls can be gotten from craft supply stores – a 6-inch ball is appropriate for a modest-sized teapot. Once you have finalized the shape, attach it to a tempered hardboard that has been cut to shape or a piece of wood using glue.

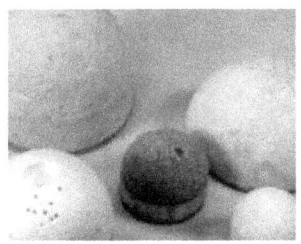

2. To form the sphere, throw a slab of clay of about ¼ to 5/16 inches thick and use toilet paper to mold and position the slab on top of the mold. Trim the lower part, take it away and repeat for the second hemisphere. Allow the hemisphere to dry.

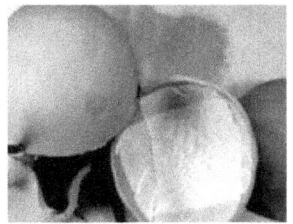

3. Roll out a coil and join it to one of the hemisphere's rim.

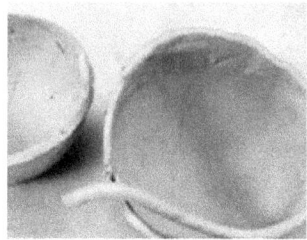

4. Join the second hemisphere with your finger or use a tool to work the seam, and with a surform tool, restructure the shape and smoothen it using a metal rib.

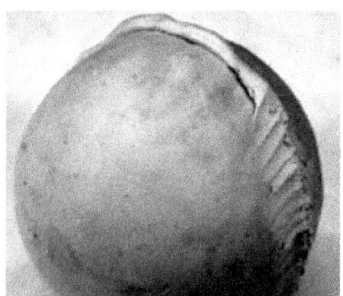 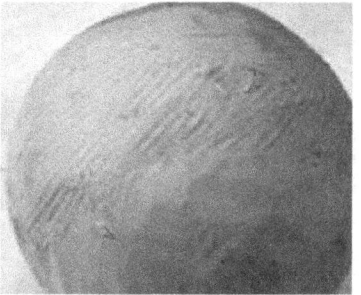

5. To form a base, use a triangular trimming tool to scoop some clay. And while the sphere sits on a plastic container that is empty, join the base to it while adding decorative elements per your style.

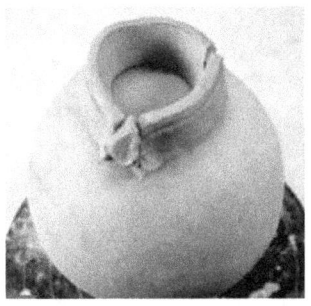

6. Once done, go on to form the lid. To do this, carve a round opening on the sphere surface, then insert toilet paper around the edge. Place a small ball of clay in the notch as shown below, then insert a coil of clay into the lid opening.

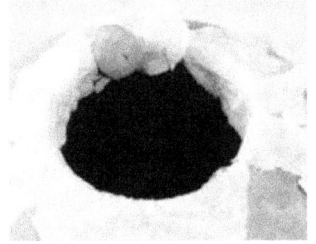 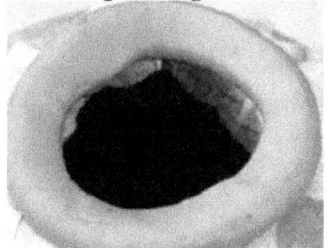

7. Take the piece of clay earlier removed and make an opening that attaches to the coil. Then turn over the lid, adding a ball of clay to its underside to help balance the lid when pouring tea.

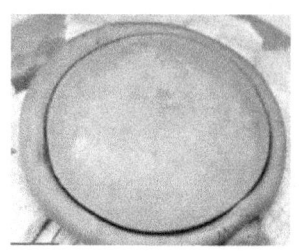 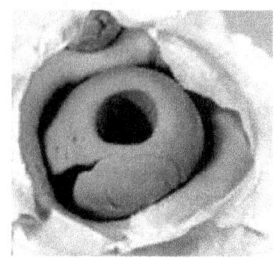

8. Proceed to create the spout and handle. The spout is formed by making a clay cone flat and using this cone to form the spout around a brush handle.

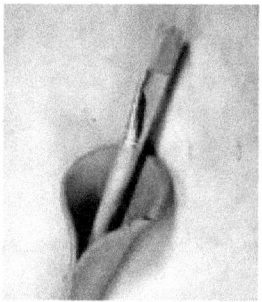

9. Trim the spout and join it to the teapot.

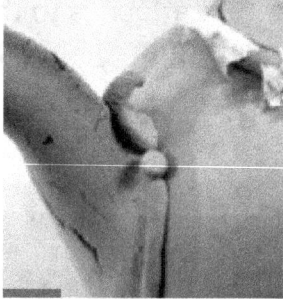

10. Use two flat dog bone shapes to form the handle

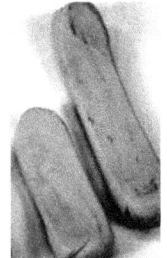

11. Assemble the handle while adding a decorative element if you choose to. The handle to the lid should be added per the same style shown below.

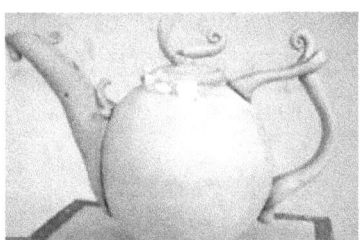 

Three-Piece Vase

Still on creating a vase, have you thought about the excitement and beauty of creating a three-piece vase? A three-piece vase is one in which three clay vases are used to form it.

Flowers can be kept in a three-piece vase, and it could serve numerous functions.

Materials

- Clay
- Calipers
- Cut off wire
- Drill bit
- Stamps

Instructions

1. Toss four pounds of clay into the shape of a bulbous of about 9 inches tall with a bowl-shaped bottom. Then give sufficient space for your hand to get inside the pot. Determine the size of the opening.

2. The piece should be attached to the bat and put aside to dry so much that it can support the top section. When the vase's body section is well

dried, a 1½-pound ball of clay should be opened all the way down to the surface of the bat and moved outward to give rise to a solid ring, forming the vase's top.

3. Calipers should be used to measure the top of this piece; this will be turned around over the vase's body. The measurement should be a little more than the opening in the vase's top body previously tossed. Afterward, use a braided cut-off wire to cut off the piece, but leave on the bat.

4. Insert the vase's body and its attached bat onto the wheel head, then turn the second bat upside down, and with caution, place it onto the top of

the body while you smoothen the joining of the two pieces. Allow it to dry sufficiently

 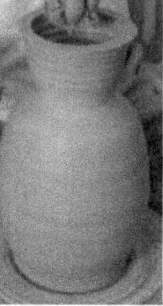

5. Trim the bottom to make it similar to the curve, then insert a slug of clay in the bottom's center and press it into place.

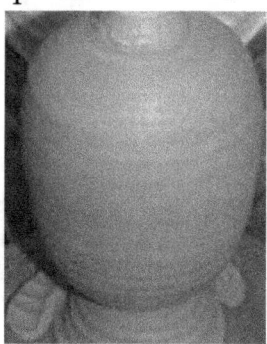

6. As the wheel turns, center the clay with some water without softening the base of the pot. Afterward, the clay should be opened in the same way you toss a new pot. Then pull a wall up and

shape into the foot. Allow it to dry well enough, and after the foot is stiffened, turn the piece right-side up.

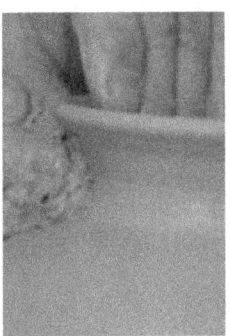

7. To add the handle, roll out a slab of clay and roll a drill bit over it for the texture. With the text facing outward, roll the clay around a pencil, remove the pencil from the clay, then attach the handle to the vase

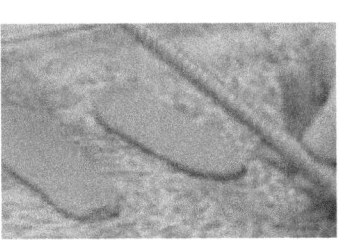

8. To improve the texture surrounding the vase's shoulder, use stamps. Clean any marks of clay with a sponge. Allow the piece to dry for several days by wrapping it around plastic.

Textured Platter

The textured platter design can be used to store things or take things from one place to another. It is also a perfect pottery design for beginners and professionals.

Materials

- Clay
- Foam
- Handmade viewfinder
- Hand tools

- Rolling pin
- Roller

Instructions

1. Smoothen out a slab and layer, then firmly pressing in objects. Texture the surface likewise.

2. Utilize stamps, found objects, and hand tools to embellish the slab.

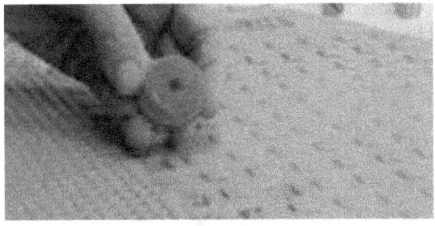

3. Proceed to roll on the top of the texture using your rolling pin. This will also make the texture soft and tuck in the marks.

4. With a handmade viewfinder, choose an exciting spot.

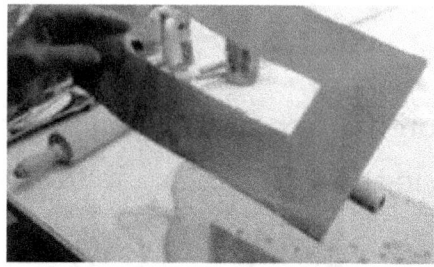

5. Cut off a dart, then using it as a pattern, cut off the other darts.

6. Raise and link the corners on the area where the darts were taken away.

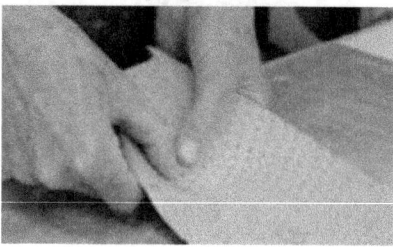

7. Take the piece and make the sides smooth using a spirit level.

8. Cut out a large triangular slab of clay and shape it into a cone form for the handles. Then raise and hit the cone three times to achieve an organic shape.

9. Ensure you slip and put the handle where it should be. Foam can also be used to support it.

10. Flip the piece to the other side using foam as its support, then fill the seams with clay to prevent cracking.

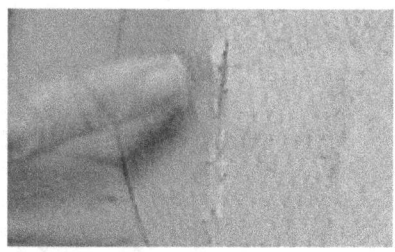

11. To make the foot, cut out a long thin piece of textured slab and place it on the bottom of the pot, shape to your desired form, then join the foot in a ring form. Also, attach the foot ring to the bottom of the serving dish. Remove excess slip using a dry brush, then blend the seam.

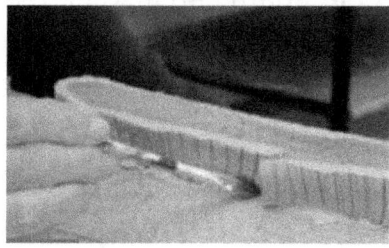

12. Use a roller to smoothen the foot while cutting decorative arches across it using a loop too.

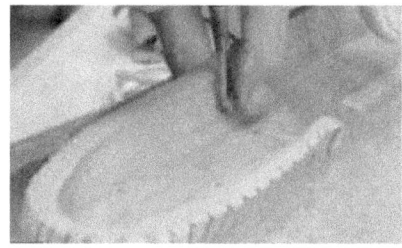

13. Bevel and finish the sides of the platter's edge using a pony roller and spirit level.

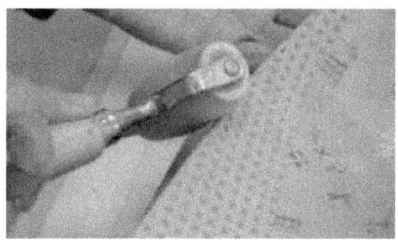

14. To finalize the piece, apply glaze firing to it. Afterward, you can design the piece as you so desire.

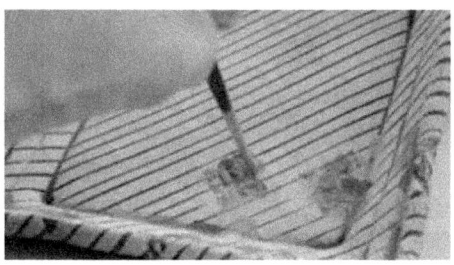

Pottery Clay Trays

You can create pottery clay trays to help you organize household items like keys and so much more.

Materials

- Sculpey clay in different colors
- Butter knife
- Rolling pin
- Shallow glass bowl
- Pen
- Scrap piece of lace
- Circular items
- Klin
- Paint

Instructions

1. Roll the clay in your hands for some minutes.

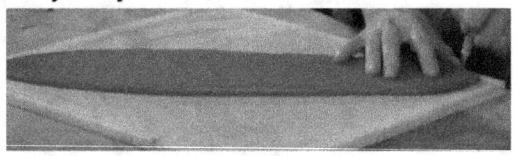

2. When it becomes soft, begin rolling it using a rolling pin to about 1/8 inch thickness.

3. Make a lace pattern. To do this, place the scrap piece on the flat clay. Then roll over the lace on few occasions with considerate force to stamp the clay.
4. Take the lace, and its pattern onto the clay.

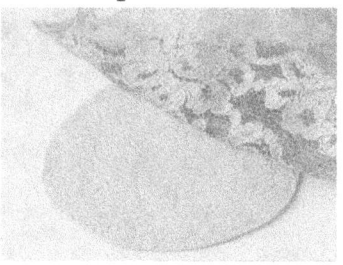

5. Make stripes and polka dots. Utilize the pen (flat end) to make a polka dot pattern in the clay. Also, create stripes by dragging a butter knife with low force over the clay.

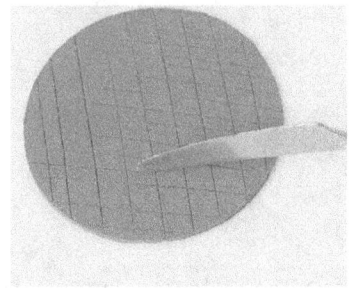

6. Trim the circles with a circular item.
7. Place the resulting circular clay into the kiln and fire it up. You can utilize a large shallow bowl as a mold to create a large piece of clay.

8. Paint if you want.

Pottery Cylindrical Pot

Are you looking to make a pottery pot with a cylinder type of design? Well, look no further as you can make cylindrical pots with clay.

Materials

- Clay
- Pottery wheel
- Sponge
- Wooden trimming tool

Instructions

1. Wedge your clay. Before moving to your wheel, you are expected to wedge your clay because it makes your clay feel compact and does not give room for air passage.

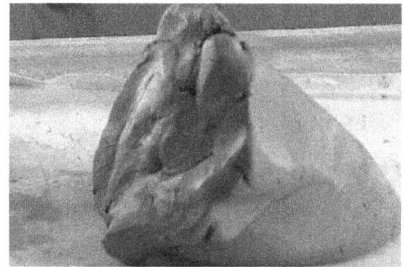

2. Position the center of the clay on the pottery wheel. Make sure you center the clay on the center of the wheel using different methods like using little pressure or allowing your wheel to move very fast.

3. Open the clay and create the lower side. While still on the pottery wheel, go on to open the clay and place your right thumb on the top and push it all the way down to form the lower side. When the process is ongoing, try to lower the wheel speed and use your left hand to support your thumb.

4. Throw the pot. Ensure your pottery wheel moves at half speed once more, but it must be lubricated as the process is ongoing.

Do this by positioning your right forefinger at the low outside of the pot and on the wheel. Supposing the clay is diverting away, simply reduce the speed of the wheel.

5. Wrap the rim. Once the pot is successfully thrown, you have to apply a few finishing touches before slicing it from the pottery wheel. Here, you are expected to use a sponge and soak the liquid content on the pot's lower part.

Proceed also to soak your chamois in the slurry for some time until it is saturated.

6. Cut the excess part of the pot. The wooden trimming tool's wedge-shaped edge should work fine to trim the outside lower part of the pot.

7. Cut the pot off the pottery wheel. This is the last step in this process. In this step, you are required to switch on the wheel rotating slow and keep the wire flush to the bat's surface and extend as much as you can.

Halt the wheel and slowly take away the bat from the head of the wheel. Position the bat away from the wheel. Once the pot is hard, carefully lift it from the bat and keep it in a safe place and make it available for bisque firing.

Coil Pot

Clay coil pots are made by carefully stacking and attaching coils of clay over another. You can choose to showcase the coil depending on what you want. It is ideal for storing items and visible contents.

Materials

- Clay
- Rolling pin
- Rib
- Wooden paddle

Instructions

1. Use a rolling pin and create a slab of clay.

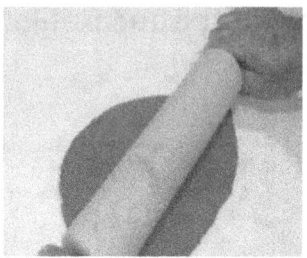

2. Proceed to cut a slab base 1/4 thick and create coils with your hand.

 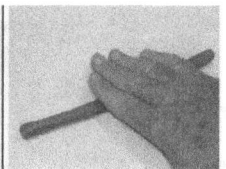

3. Score and slip base and add coil before pinching the coil into a slab on the inner part.

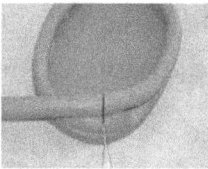 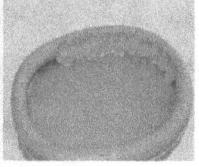

4. Attach coils with your two hands and perform the same on the exterior side.

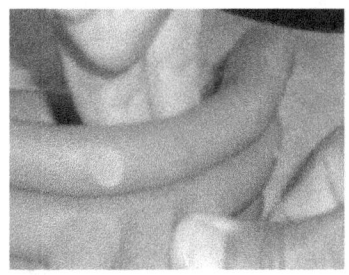

5. Utilize the rib to smooth the pinched coil and position the second coil before smudging the coil in the lower coil side.

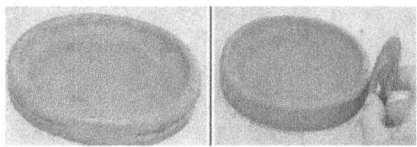

6. Continue adding layers and attach the coils in different positions.

7. Utilize a longer coil to increase the pot and go through the same process once more.
8. Coil and pinch the rim before concluding your pot.

9. With a wooden paddle, proceed to shape your pot to the design you want and fire glaze it.

Pottery Starfish

The pottery clay starfish project is usually designed for mounting on the wall. Both beginners and professionals can take up this project.

Materials

- Rolling pin
- Template

- Clay

Instructions

1. With a rolling pin, smoothen and press the slab.

2. Then make a paper template before tracing the template on the clay slab.
3. Spot the clay on the template and slice the starfish pattern.

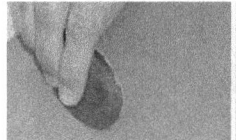

4. Position it on the top of the hump mold and push it to shape.
5. Change it to a little hump mold and push the clay to the little shape.
6. Make the starfish arms and take away the hump mold.

7. Go through and create another one before making the surface flat.

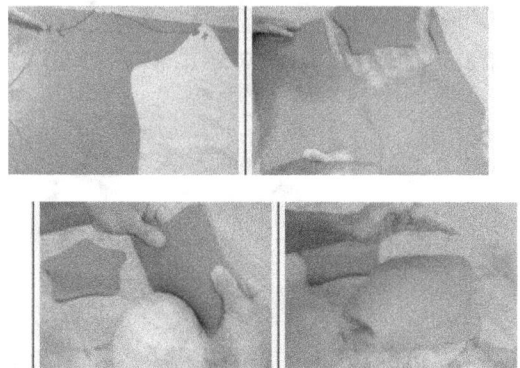

8. Score the entire contact pint and slip the entire one.
9. Join two halves and link the two sides.
10. Blend it using a wooden tool and create a small coil.

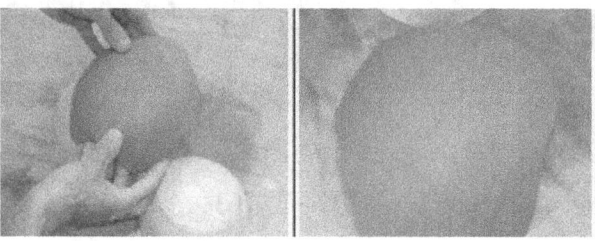

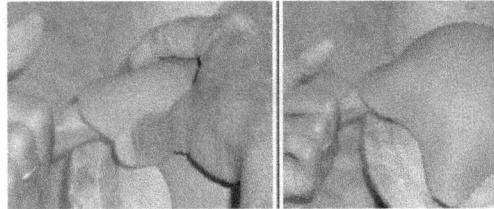

11. Proceed to make the coil flat before positioning it around the contact point.
12. Include extra coil and blend it.

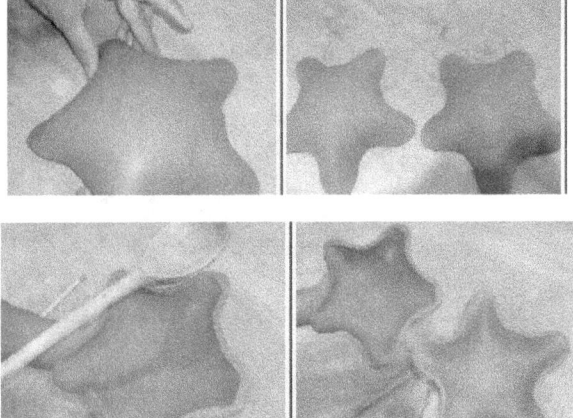

13. Use a rib to smoothen the coil and take a sponge to change the shape.

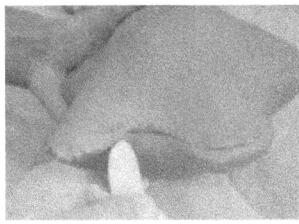

14. With a sponge, form arms extension and shape it.

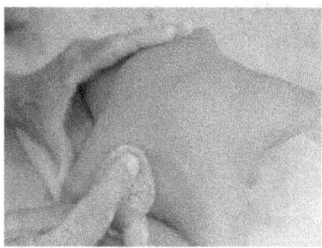

15. Create a hole for air to pass out and link the extension.

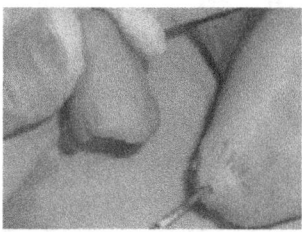

16. From there, you can blend, include a coil, blend coil, shape arm, include extra definition, form texture, and conclude your clay starfish.

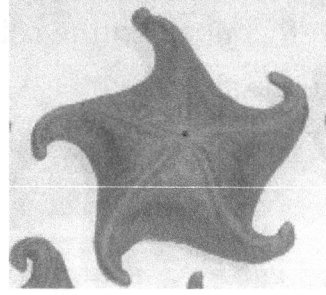

Water Font Clay

As a beginner, you can start designing pottery designs by creating a water font clay project.

Materials

- Clay
- Template
- Newspaper
- Miter

Instructions

1. First of all, utilize the template to slice the slab to your preferred size.
2. Then smoothen the surface using a red mud rib.

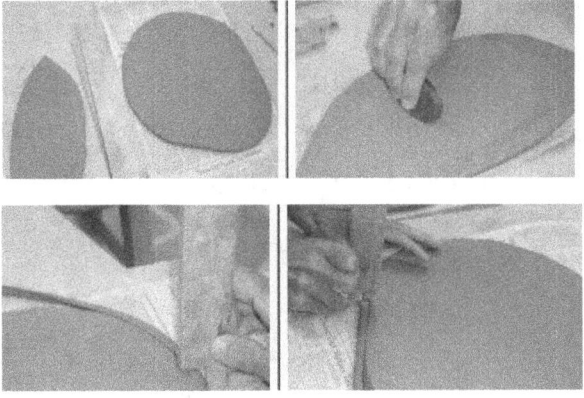

3. Furthermore, use a muter to bevel corners to about 30 degrees.
4. Bevel the spot where the 2nd piece is supposed to be attached.
5. Proceed to miter the other slab and score the beveled corners.

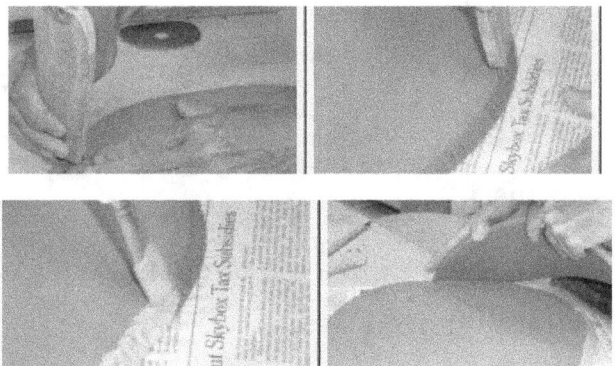

6. Slip the scored corners and join the two sides.
7. Position the clay symmetrically and move the curve. Then use the coil to make sure the attachment is the stick.

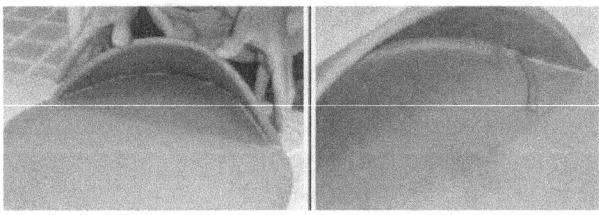

8. Once your joint is done, simply mark and start scalloping the edge.
9. Scallop the rim more and push the scalloped rim to your preferred angle.

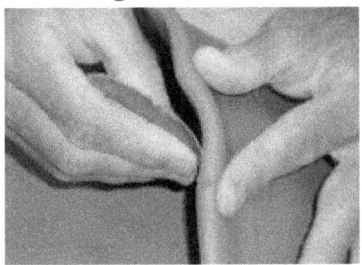

10. Define the scallop to the best length and join leaves if you want.

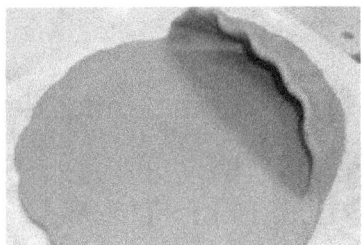

Slab-Built Pottery Mug

The essence of the slab-built pottery mug is to store liquid contents and other items. Within a few hours, you should be done with creating a slab pottery mug.

Materials

- Water
- Clay (1 pound)
- Food-safe glaze
- Pottery needle
- Klin
- Small paintbrush
- String
- Jar
- Modeling tool
- Ruler

Instructions

1. Make or organize the mug floor. To get an altogether cylindrical mug, you should begin with a circular floor. The best way to get this done is to use a glass or jar to act as a circle template. Furthermore, the mug wall will join the upper part of the floor, making the circle large to contain the wall's thickness and your preferred inner mug diameter.

From there, take out your clay slab to about 1/4 inch thickness. Then position your jab in the center of the slab. With your pottery needle, you can cut around the jar leading inside the clay. Lastly, remove the remaining clay

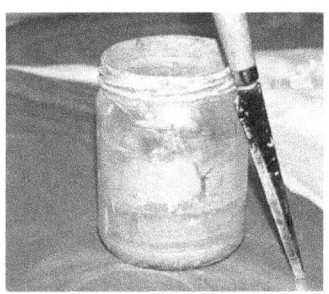

2. Form and join the wall of the mug. You need to create the mug wall. To do this, utilize a piece of string to calculate the mug floor's circumference (This should be done to know how long your wall slab will be).

Next, choose the height you want your mug to reach before rolling out your clay slab to a similar thickness your mug floor also has. Then utilize a ruler to measure the rectangle in the clay slab.

The measurement is expected to be a bit longer than the mug floor's circumference, and the width should have the same length as the height. Trim the triangle and remove the remaining clay.

Supposing the clay has lost its thickness, permit the wall slab to become hard before proceeding. Then join the wall to the floor and also join the sides to form the cylindrical shape of the body of the mug. You can press the entire sides together (inner and outer mug).

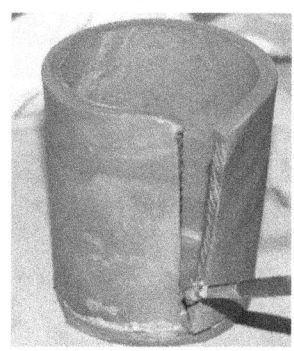

3. Make the mug's handle. To obtain a strap handle, take out a clay slab with a similar thickness as the mug wall and floor. Then measure and trim a slab with the width and height you want but don't forget that it will shrink a bit when it is dried and placed in the kiln.

4. Join the handle to the mug. Attach the handle and the mug and weld them. Since mug handles are hard to attach, ensure your joints are also strong.

Once you've done the above, you only need to do some added work like rounding the rim.

5. Roundup. Transform your slab-built mug to ceramic by using bisque firing. After firing, glaze the mug with a food-safe glaze, and you will find the inner part glossy and the rim hard to form a smooth texture.

Lastly, leave to dry before using.

Basic Slab Pot

The basic slab pot design is perfect for beginners, although a high concentration level is needed to make the design as attractive as possible.

Materials

- Water
- Clay
- Pottery needle
- Klin
- Small paintbrush
- String
- Modeling tool

- Ruler

Instructions

1. Create a slab. Make a thick slurry slab before you proceed with the next step and leave it to dry first. Make small pots, firmly press the slabs, wrap a large amount of clay inside a ball, and use your hands to make it smooth and flat.

    Large pots require you to roll out the slabs with a rolling pin.

    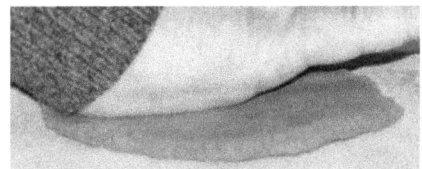

2. Make the base of your slab pot. With the potter's needle, cut a bit of the slab you made. Make it into any size you want. Then slowly smoothen the trimmed corners by tapping each corner.

    You can also use the needle to make the top part of the slab along each corner. Do not make it deeper than 1/16 inch and wider than 1/4 inch.

3. Make the first and second slab pot sides. Make a slab and also cut one corner into a straight line with your potter's needle. Further, cut away the remaining clay to have a similar width. Proceed to cut the top corner to the height you want, make the second slab, and place it to similar measurements.

4. Join the first two sides. Score the lower corner of the side slab. While on the side that will act as the inner part of the completed pit, score the inner

surface along the two side edges. With your brush, slowly brush a line of slurry on the edge of the base slab.

Roll out a small coil and place it along into the side and base slabs' inner edge. Go through this same step for the second side slab.

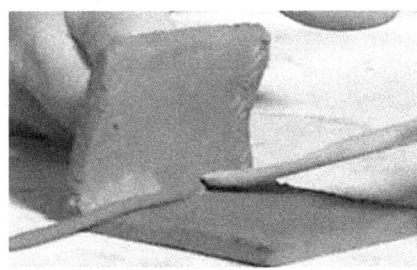

5. Make the final two sides. By following the steps in the previous step, you can create the final two sides of the slab pot.

6. Join the last two sides. Score the lower part and the side corners of any of the slabs. Then with

your brush, casually brush a line of slurry in the scoring on every edge.

Proceed to place any remaining coil from joining the first two slabs to raise the coil to reach the side joint. Go through this same process for the final side slab and ensure that you score the inner surface.

7. Conclude your slab pot and dry it. To prevent your pot from breaking, lightly weld the exterior surface of every joint with a round wooden tool. Also, do not fire the clay until you are sure it is bone-dry. After drying your pot, take it to the bisque to fire it up and place it in the kiln for firing.

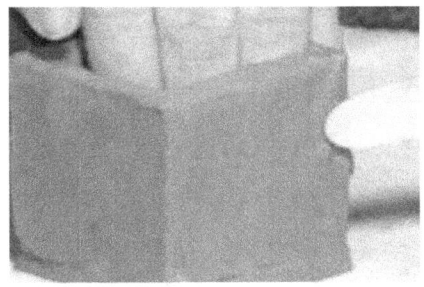

Ceramic Plant Pot

Beautiful pots and plant vessels create an amazing style, and it is a perfect way to add more beauty to your home. It is a beginner project that can be made with virtually any color.

Materials

- Clay
- Klin
- Bisque fire
- Damp sponge

Instructions

1. Begin with a small ball of compressed clay. Here, you can decide on the size of the plant pot you want. After deciding on the size, you need to

ensure your clay is compressed and all manner of air taken away. This will save it from exploding in the kiln. After compressing it, roll it to form a smooth round ball.

2. Push your thumb in the middle. Proceed to push your thumb using your smooth round ball into the center and ensure you don't push all the way through. After this, you will get your base.

3. Keep on pressing. Continue the process of pressing the center of your pot with your thumb

and index finger. Additionally, you can also create equal pinches.

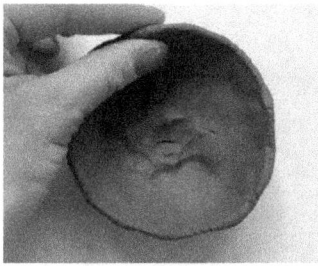

4. Smooth the entire pot. The next step is to smooth the whole pot. With a damp sponge, smooth the whole pot. Leave it to dry, and after that, you can take it to the bisque firing. This will change the ware into a porous manner for glazing.

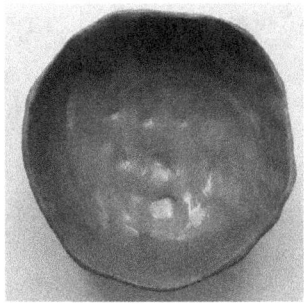

5. Bisque fire and glaze your pot. Remove your pots from the kiln and cool them. At this time, they

will be sufficient for glazing. Once the glaze firing is done, you can proceed to complete your pot.

Clay Plate

Are you looking to serve food with the use of a clay plate? We have just the perfect answer as we will show you how to create an air-dried clay plate for serving.

Materials

- Air-dry clay
- Rolling pin
- Knife
- Spray varnish
- Acrylic paintbrushes
- Newspaper

Instructions

1. First of all, roll the clay with a rolling pin.

2. From there, you can create different types of plates, like a pineapple-shaped plate or a watermelon-shaped plate.

3. Turn the trims of the plate using your hand and leave it to dry.

4. Use the acrylic paint and paint the designs you want, and allow it to dry.

Clay and Rope Pot

Designs just even got better with the making of the clay and rope pot. In this design, the bottom part is made of clay, while the pot's top is knitted with ropes. It is also an easy design you can carry out.

Materials

- Bowl
- Thin straw
- Needle
- Rope
- Clay

- Roller

Instructions

1. Roll the clay and slowly take it into the bowl. Then press the clay using your fingers and take the excess clay to a particular side.

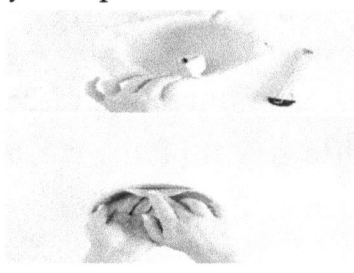

2. Trim the excessive clay and find a little bowl of water and begin smoothing the rough sides.
3. With a flat end thin straw, create holes close to the bowl's edges and allow it to dry.

4. Once dried, take out the pot from the bowl and smoothen it with a wet sponge and allow it to dry.

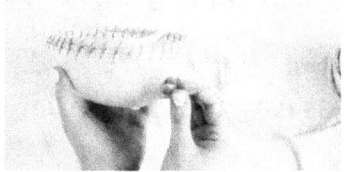

5. Cut the long thread and knit on the needle. Proceed to sew it on the created holed and get to the final layer.

Clay Spoon

This is usually a kitchen utensil used for stirring or taking out something from the pot. It is easy to make, and you can do so in simple steps.

Materials

- Clay
- Paint
- Objects for the handle

Instructions

1. Roll out the clay and form a little bowl, which will act as the spoon.

2. Create the handles differently by using objects.

3. Attach the handle and bowl and leave it to dry.

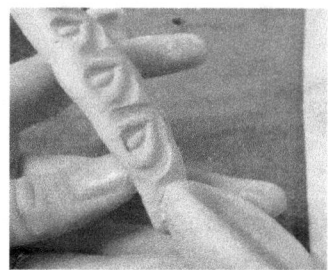

4. Proceed to paint the spoon with any color of your choice and remove the excessive underglaze.

Chapter 7

Fixing Common Pottery Mistakes

As a beginner or even an expert, you are prone to mistakes in all areas of life, and even as a potter. However, it's not advisable to dwell on these errors when you can easily find a solution and fix the mistake.

Common mistakes like over-firing are bound to happen, especially if we are eager to get our first pottery design ready for sale or storage. The term "glazing" is used to describe a pottery design that looks extremely beautiful and completed.

Its job is to leave a coating on your pot and push it to stay for a long time. A wrong glazing work can destroy your pottery design, which can be challenging as a beginner or expert.

In this section, we have compiled the common pottery mistakes and the solutions that accompany them:

1. **Under firing**

This is clearly the opposite of over firing, and it is not good for pottery. Under firing simply means not firing your clay to the extent that it takes in heat.

When you fire clay, It should be done to reach a certain level to derive the glazing on the entire pottery surface. Because of this, you should try as much as possible not to under fire. As a result of under firing, you will get a scratchy glaze surface and dryness. Additionally, it may also result in cracks on the glaze surface.

If you want to prevent under firing your clay, you must maintain or keep up with the glazing temperature and time. Nonetheless, the under firing can be corrected easily when you fire it once again but at a much-increased temperature that helps rescue the glaze once more.

2. Over firing

When inserting your pottery design into the kiln, you must know the right proportion of firing it needs. If you fire more, you are simply adding to the durability and perfectness of the glazing surface. Meanwhile, when we talk about the firing, we do not mean you should fire your pottery too much because it has its consequences.

The reason over firing is not advisable is that it results from glazing liquefied. Over firing leads to the glaze becoming thin at the upper part and the lower side thick, which means the glazing won't be leveled.

Going further, the glaze might drip down on the kiln that leads to a grave mistake. Likewise, pitting and pin holding might happen at the upper glaze part because of over firing.

Potters may also have to study and focus on the amount of temperature the glaze seen on your pot can contain. You should also be aware of the number of times you have to fire your pot and endeavor not to fire it. The most recommended way to stop over firing is to use a glaze that contains a maturation level of two, three, or four cones.

3. **Uneven glaze proportions**

The addition of glazing should be done by using the right proportion of materials to prevent the issues led by uneven glazing.

Here are some of the outcomes of uneven glazing and how to correct the issues. They include:

- **Shivering:** Raise the alkaline and Feldspar materials and reduce glaze silica.
- **Crazing:** You can solve this issue by reducing the Feldspar and other materials and raising the addition of Silica, Lead Oxide, Boron, Alumina and more that contain potassium or Sodium in the gas mixture body.
- **Blisters:** Reduce flux materials such as Boric Acid, Sodium carbonate. Potassium carbonate, Sulfate, and Magnesium.
- **Pin and pitting holing:** Erase the zinc content, increasing the length time of the firing cycle, holding the kiln at the glaze temperature for a short time, gradually cooling the kiln, raising the temperature of maturation, and applying the right glaze layer can assist in managing the issues.

4. Blebbing

This is also another mistake commonly made that ruins glazing and potteries. To achieve smooth and amazing glazing or surface, you should endeavor to prevent blebbing.

The term **"Blebbing"** is caused by air pockets seen on the clay surface. Blebbing mostly takes place when preparing the pottery clay.

Glazing faults such as pin holing, pitting, and blistering might take place in blebbing.

5. Applying glaze the wrong way

While making pots, most people often make the mistake of applying glaze the wrong way. As a beginner potter, you must be watchful and take precautionary measures when applying glaze to your finished pottery work.

In some cases, glaze on pottery work in a small manner can result in discoloration and rough glazing. The lack of glazing level leads to splotching and streaking of the pot temperature and also results to.

6. Too much powdery glazing

When organizing glaze for pottery, it is important not to apply excessive powder. Crawling is identified as the major issue that happens when glazing is done. To halt your glazing to change into a crawled one, you have to lessen your powder glaze use.

In fact, most people have suggested that you should use a liquid type of glaze to prevent issues such as crawling. Lastly, endeavor not to apply another phase of glaze on a dried surface glaze.

7. Poor adhesion

The glaze you want to apply on the pot must have the right type of adherence inside it. If not, it will result in inappropriate glazing on your pottery design. Furthermore, the application of glazing in an inappropriate way has a big say in arriving at poor adhesion.

Additionally, the absence of adherence leads to the glaze crawling. This is why it is best to avoid it to prevent the manifestation of inaccurate and unleveled pot glazing.

To solve the poor adhesion issue, the pot you want to apply your glaze must be washed, cleaned and left to dry. Once done, you need to apply a glaze to it. Do not also forget that you need to be cautious about the coating level drying so that your glaze won't fade away.

8. Poor-fitting on the clay

The glazing being applied on top of the pottery design must fit perfectly and ideally on the clay's body. The fitting challenges will come up when the applied glaze is excessive or too small compared to the clay's body. Meanwhile, when the firing begins to happen, the melting glaze has to be done the right way on the clay's body, affecting the cooling of the kiln or pots.

Additionally, the growth level of the clay and glaze might be different in some situations. When this happens, you have to calculate the right expansion measurements and know the clay and size's contraction and expansion capacity. This is why it is advisable to know some things about the materials and fluxes before going on to glaze. It will save you from the problem of placing imperfect fitting.

9. Accidents happening in the kiln

We are humans, and accidents such as breaking of kiln shelves, leaning of pieces, breaking pot edges, and so much more are bound to happen in some situations. More accidents that can happen include dipping glaze inside other pots or staining colors in different pots. All these issues and challenges can stop you from achieving the result you wanted.

So, how can the listed problems be solved? The best you can do is to be careful and watchful when undergoing the coloring and firing process. It is important to be careful and carry out the pot making process with caution and patience to arrive at your desired outcome.

The end... almost!

Hey! We've made it to the final chapter of this book, and I hope you've enjoyed it so far.

If you have not done so yet, I would be incredibly thankful if you could take just a minute to leave a quick review on Amazon

Reviews are not easy to come by, and as an independent author with a little marketing budget, I rely on you, my readers, to leave a short review on Amazon.

Even if it is just a sentence or two!

So if you really enjoyed this book, please...

\>\> Click here to leave a brief review on Amazon.

I truly appreciate your effort to leave your review, as it truly makes a huge difference.

Chapter 8

Pottery Making Frequently Asked Questions (Q&A)

Are you looking to make pottery designs using clay? Well, we have compiled some of the most frequently asked questions about pottery making.

Look below to see the pottery making frequently asked questions prepared for you:

Q - How is clay explained?

Ans - Clay is identified as a normally happening set of minerals with fine molecule size. Clay normally holds liquid, solidifies water when dried and heated, and also holds its shape well when framed and extended. Its ability to stretch is identified as plasticity.

By training and practicing, you can figure out how to toss pottery clay into useful tasks and afterward fire them to solidify them.

Q - What does a clay body mean?

Ans - Clay bodies allude to the attachment of clay dependent on its fixings. Various activities require diverse clay bodies and hence various sums and sorts of fixings.

Q - Wedging is defined as?

Ans - Wedging is the act of working with ceramics mud to eliminate air bubbles, blend it to consistency, and adjust the dirt particles to help in wheel tossing.

There are two primary kinds of wedging: namely table wedging and spiral kneading.

Q - Spiral kneading is defined as?

Ans - Spiral kneading blends and eliminates the air from clay by extending and squeezing it into a table. Once the clay is pivoted, it takes on a twisting shape.

Q - How can I restructure dry and old clay?

Ans - This is a typical question asked by several people, and it is a decent one. Initially, start by separating it into little pieces. Then place it in a pail and add water until it simply rounds the clay. Allow it to saturate for a couple of days so that the clay will become soft.

When soft, you would then be able to utilize a blender appended to a force drill, or even only a hefty stick. Alternatively, you can use anything to mix the clay. Mix the slurry blend until it is all around diversified. You should not make it excessively runny but only such as pancake batter. Meanwhile, if it is excessively runny, you may have to add some more clay to make it hard and afterward let it in the water some more.

In the end, place your batter onto a mortar bat or into a cushion case or other texture. The explanation behind the mortar or texture is that it will assimilate and wick the dampness away from the mud all the more rapidly. It should dry like this for about a day or more.

Ensure you check it frequently. When it draws near to a more sticky consistency, the time has come to wedge it completely. Whenever you have wedged it completely, it is prepared to toss on the clay wheel.

Make sure you wedge it well and set it back until you're prepared to utilize it. You can, in a real sense, store pottery clay for quite a long time.

Q - How can I take away glue or old adhesive from clay?

Ans - The initial stage in eliminating old glue is to figure out what kind of cement it is. It could be water-based glue, super paste, or contact concrete.

There are strategies to eliminate the old glue, but you must first know the following:

1. What paste is it?
2. Is the material the paste is applied to absorbent or non-permeable?
3. What kind of equipment is accessible to you?

For your notice, Non-permeable material includes: Porcelain, china, stoneware, metal, while Permeable material includes: Earthware, stone, mortar, wood

Ways to remove:

1. Dissolvable
2. Hot water
3. Light
4. Mechanical partition by cutting the patched part
5. Kiln furnace

With a sharp item, hit the old cement. If it can be moved, it is undoubtedly not Epoxy and might be broken up.

Now, let's go through the first four strategies listed above to remove glue from clay.

1. How to use solvent

Go through the steps below to use solvent:

1. While in an open room and wearing a veil, soak the solidified regions with Acetone and hang tight for a few minutes or until you notice softening.
2. If the cemented areas don't move away from each other, apply force to do so.
3. Scratch off the soft cement and wipe the tops using alcohol.

NOTE: Before applying the Acetone, ensure you do a little experiment on your item to confirm that the Acetone won't destroy your thing. Acetone will immediately harm any polymer-based item. Use all safety guidelines for utilizing Acetone, and don't skip any.

If you are not careful, the disintegrated cement may assimilate and stain permeable surfaces.

2. Hot Water

A large number of glues will always soften after they are inundated in hot water.

Go through the below steps to use boiling water:

1. Whenever you are firing up the ceramic in water, don't drop the thing in bubbling water to stay away from breaks because of warm stun. Position the clay object in room temperature water and begin the warming with the item in the water.
2. Leave it to boil for at least 3 minutes, check the item to know whether the solidified parts are isolated or isolated with light pressing. If it does, simply use heat gloves to hold the hot thing and with extremely sharp steel, while hot, eliminate the excess epoxy.
3. Grinding using a metal brush might be needed if excess epoxy is still there.
4. Erase or wipe out surfaces using alcohol.

Likely side effect: The dissolved glue may retain and stain porous surfaces.

3. Light

This technique requires insight with using light and applying the fire on the top without causing harm.

Go through the steps below to use light:

1. Fire the covered regions with a nonstop motion and with the fire not very near the surface.
2. The warmed regions need to construct temperature consistently.
3. Apply force to isolate the fortified areas.
4. When isolated, pick up a metallic brush or grind to eliminate the cement.
5. Wipe away the dirt surfaces with alcohol.

Likely side effect: Heat packing up in a particular area can lead to breaking.

NOTE: Ensure you use it in an open space and protect your eye.

4. Mechanical partition by cutting the patched part

Having plaster items or when all other option does not work out, you can adopt this strategy.

The direst outcome imaginable is the point at which the old glue was utilized on permeable materials. For example, earthenware, stone, or mortar. The old glue douses into the material's porous surface, and the full profundity of entrance requires granulating.

The steps to use this strategy are outlined below:

1. Utilize a Dremel cutting to slice through the repaired line.
2. When isolated, granulate or pick up a metallic brush to eliminate them.
3. Erase surfaces with alcohol.

Likely side effect: Cutting eliminates the glues, yet it likewise eliminates a portion of the vessel's material, which impacts the messed up pieces' fit, and this needs extra fill, extra sanding, additional painting, accordingly, more intricate fix.

NOTE: Ensure it is utilized in an open space and with safety glasses.

Q - What is crazing, and for what reason do they occur?

Ans - You can find a group of lines or breaks in the heated coated surface. For the most part, they happen toward the oven end heating process when the external surface becomes warm before the pottery clay under the coating starts becoming warm.

Crazing can further occur during the vessel's existence because of fast temperature alterations such as boiling water to cool water.

Q - Crazed coating achieved purposefully; what should I not carry out?

Ans –

1. First of all, don't utilize chlorine or dye. The reason is that it might eliminate the stains yet additionally can harm your fired item.

2. Never warm in stove. Assuming the stain contains ancient oil, it can dissolve and extend under the coating, making a bigger stain.

Here's what you should carry out instead

Purchase ordinary oxygen dye normally used for washing clothes. Then blend the powder in steaming hot water and sit tight for it to become warm. Finally,

Absorb your stained object inside the solution for a few hours or until the entire stain disappears.

Check below for a more proven method:

Visit a drug store and buy 8% Hydrogen peroxide dye that is normally used to dye hair. Proceed to absorb your stained object in the solution for some time. At that point, while it is still wet, simply position it in a stove and set it to 180 to 200 degrees Fahrenheit (82 - 93 C). Allow the stove to ascend to 180-200 degrees F.

NOTE: Never make the mistake of placing your object in a preheated oven. The quick temperature adjustment is capable of breaking the object off a few portions of the crazed coating. After 30 to 1 hour, remove it and sit tight to turn warm before washing it with room temperature water. You may find somewhat shaded water leaking out from the crazing washing.

Even though this process eliminates the color, it doesn't eliminate the unfamiliar matter like dirt leading to staining. Subsequently, a stain can return whenever there is moisture around.

Another point to note is that using a harder arrangement of peroxide is very hazardous. It can consume the skin and cause lasting harm. Offer the more grounded hydrogen peroxide work to the experts.

Q - What should I do if the stain is not removed?

Ans – When it comes to difficult stains, you should endeavor to go through the listed processes every day by using new materials.

Q - Why do people not go through the above steps of removing stains?

Ans -

1. The outcomes are not ensured and cannot be guessed.
2. Potential coating chipping is likely to happen.
3. All the listed processes might not eliminate the material that resulted in the formation of the bacteria, and there is every chance a similar pollutant will resurface.
4. Decolorizing may not eliminate inorganic stains, like rust. For this situation, the stain should be eliminated with reclamation exertion and extensive fix.

Q - About coat creeping?

Ans - Creeping is the place where the liquid coating pulls out into a separate place, leaving uncovered clay patches. The edges of the islands are thickened and easily adjusted.

In moderate cases, there are a couple of exposed patches of clay, while in extreme cases, the coating structures dots on the mud surface and trickles off onto the rack. The issue is generally common in the once-fired product.

Q - Is the coating contracting a lot during drying?

Ans - Assuming the dried coating structures breaks, it is an indication that the coating is contracting excessively. These separation points give spots to the sliding to begin. There are various potential ways to fix this?

- If exceptionally fine-particle materials are available (for example, zinc, bone debris), these will add to higher shrinkage during drying. You can use calcined zinc, engineered bone.
- It is entirely expected to see 20% clay. Meanwhile, if the entire one is available, you can operate with less plastic clay.

- If a coating has been ball processed for a really long time, it might shrink too much. Alternatively, profoundly ground coatings may create a cushioned set down.

Q - Is the coating drying excessively sluggish?

Ans –

- If the coating dries very fast, the most delicate phases of attachment are expanded, and breaks in the dried coating layer can show up. Air pockets in the wet coating layer can likewise shape during the drying process; these become regions of no bond with the fundamental body and, in this way, can induce creeping during softening.

  This can happen if a product is slight, and the coat has high water content, or if a product is now wet when the coating is applied. To accelerate drying, you can preheat it to 150C or more if required.

Q - Is the product once-fire?

Ans -

- Once-heated product is considerably more inclined to slipping because the mechanical coating body bond is harder to accomplish and keep up. If the coating is applied to hard products, it should recoil with the body.

During the beginning phases of firing the product, the experience volume will change and the compound changes that create gases. As a result, it will make it hard for the coating to hold tight.

- When a coating is applied to hard products, you should have the option to tune its reduction by changing the original one and sums of the clay in the formula. Endeavor to estimate this process.
- The once-fire products should not be fired up excessively fast, particularly through the water-smoking period. Ensure the product is totally dry before the firing process commences.

Q - How to forestall a clogged-up clay sink?

Ans - One of the clay studio issues is keeping sinks clog-up free to remove the channel to forestall seepage issues. The associated technique includes:

- Simple to actualize
- Simple to keep up
- Doesn't require enough space beneath the sink
- Requires you to pay a couple of dollars.

Not to worry because we have utilized this studio sink channel trap technique. What you need to get is a 5-7" pipe and adhere to directions as explained below:

Add a piece of line in the channel - the line needs to firmly fit the sink's channel opening. The wastewater should fill the sink. Consequently, the sink will top off until the water level arrives at the line's summit, and it makes its way to the line into the channel. The pottery clay particles are thicker than water and will remain in the lower part of the sink.

Conclusion

This is just a concise outline of the pottery craftsmanship, art and history. Pottery, alongside large numbers of different crafts, is best taught with active experience.

Even though it requires some investment and time to gain proficiency in the art, it is still satisfying and worthwhile to use clays and turn them into beautiful works of art, and I hope that this book has been invaluable in helping you do so.

I wish you all the best.

www.ingramcontent.com/pod-product-compliance
Lightning Source LLC
Chambersburg PA
CBHW050318120526
44592CB00014B/1955